CHER HAMPTON

Set Boundaries & Change Your Life

Life-Changing Strategies to Set Healthy Boundaries in Relationships, Start Saying No, and Be Assertive

Contents

BONUS: Your Free Gifts

I'm only offering these bonuses for FREE to my readers. This is a way of saying thanks for your purchase. In this gift, you will find a self-development course and a guide with extra tools to start your inner journey.

The Personality Development Wisdom Course

Inside this theoretical and video course, you will find:

1. Personality Development - An Overview
2. How to Transform Yourself into a Better Version
3. How To Improve Your Body Language
4. How to Boost Up Your Self-Confidence, Self-Esteem, and Motivation
5. Best Tips to Overcome Procrastination
6. The Power of Positive Thinking
7. How to Improve Your Workplace Wellness
8. How to Enhance Your Softskill
9. Learn and Practice the Art of Work-Life Balance
10. How to Deal With Failures
11. How to Manage and Overcome Your Fears
12. Best Ways to Deal With Difficult People
13. Stress and Energy Management
14. How to Have a Productive Day
15. Bonus 1 - Cheat Sheet
16. Bonus 2 - Mind Map
17. Bonus 3 - Top Resource Report
18. Bonus 4 - 10 Extra Articles

Healing your Inner Child First Guide

Inside this book, you'll discover:

1. How to use journaling in the healing process.
2. Questions to remember your Inner Child.
3. Space to write your thoughts down.
4. Questions to better understand your Inner Child's pain.
5. Motivational things to say to your Inner Child.
6. Positive affirmations + 5-step method to make your own.
7. An extra Inner Child meditation.
8. A checklist.
9. And more...

To receive this **bonus,** go to: https://booksforbetterlife.com/innerchild

Or scan the QR code:

Introduction

"You are not required to set yourself on fire to keep others warm."

— UNKNOWN

Pouring From an Empty Cup

I was raised in what many refer to as a dysfunctional home environment. My mother and biological father went separate ways when I was one year old, and so I was raised by my mother and stepfather.

As young as I was, I felt responsible to take care of my parents and do whatever I could to make them happy since they both battled with mental health issues. My mother was diagnosed with bipolar disorder and my stepfather suffered from depression. Sadly, when I was seven years old, my stepfather lost his battle with depression and committed suicide.

From that moment onward, I told myself that my mother's well-being would become my priority. An enormous amount of guilt came over me for being the "lucky one" who didn't seem to be fighting inner demons. I felt that the only way not to feel as guilty was to sacrifice my time, energy, and well-being at the expense of taking care of others.

By the time I hit my teenage years, I was burned out and suffering from depression. The irony is that I didn't think I needed anyone to take care of me. I had convinced myself that my feelings and life experiences weren't as urgent as my family members'. I kept pouring into other people's cups, until eventually, I ran dry.

Finally, I had reached my breaking point and knew deep down that something had to change.

If you're reading this book, you might experience or know someone who experiences difficulties setting boundaries in relationships. Your story might look and sound different from mine, but we have one thing in common: We've both struggled to say 'no' at some point in our lives. For some reason, we grew up thinking that saying no to others might jeopardize the relationship or cause them to reject us. Since we couldn't risk losing them, we decided to hide or deny our own needs and desires.

As a qualified developmental psychologist, I often use my own life story as an analogy for what a lack of boundaries during early childhood leads to. In general, babies are able to start learning rules when they reach the 12-month milestone, and by four years old, the child can start learning about limits, choices, and consequences.

However, when a child is raised in a dysfunctional home environment where one or both parents are not emotionally available to enforce healthy discipline, reward good behavior, and offer positive reinforcement, the child grows up feeling unprepared to face the world. They may not have the proper mental and emotional tools to cultivate a healthy self-esteem and build mutually beneficial and safe relationships.

This book is dedicated to the grown-ups that were robbed of those early childhood lessons about setting boundaries and filling your own cup first. You will learn how to identify your emotional triggers and poor coping strategies that have been making it difficult to set healthy limits with others. You will also learn how to challenge that inner critic that feeds you fear-based beliefs about yourself and others, which causes you to feel afraid to stand up for yourself.

It took me many years to reach a point where I felt comfortable with being disliked, overlooked, or misunderstood. But the truth is, I would have never healed from my people-pleasing ways if I didn't get started on my journey. You can think of this book as the beginning of your own healing journey, too. You have the opportunity to work through deep insecurities that have been holding you back from living a fulfilling life, and redefine how you wish to live!

Are you ready to set boundaries and ultimately change your life for the better? If so, keep reading.

1

Living Within Boundaries

"Daring to set boundaries is about having the courage to love ourselves even when we risk disappointing others."

— BRENE BROWN

This chapter talks about:

- The benefits of setting healthy boundaries
- The difference between loose, rigid, and healthy boundaries
- Six types of boundaries to set in different areas of your life

Putting Up a Door, Not a Wall

The subject of setting boundaries is always a difficult one. Many of us grew up believing that boundaries were an aggressive way to keep others at bay. We saw setting boundaries as being the same as putting up walls, and since we didn't want to isolate ourselves from others, we thought that these walls were unnecessary.

Adults who experience a difficult time setting boundaries typically grew up in households where expressing a sense of self or having the freedom to voice ideas or concerns was shunned. Some parents may have explicitly said, "Your opinions, thoughts, and feelings don't matter," and others may have implicitly suggested it through their behaviors.

For these adults, creating limits with others or saying the word 'no' was therefore treated as an exception, not the norm. Unless they were severely under pressure, under-resourced, or exhausted to the point of barely moving their bodies, their answer would always be 'yes' and they would tolerate whatever attitudes or behaviors others decided to express toward them.

I used to be a kid afraid of disappointing others. This was partly due to my highly sensitive nature, where instead of checking in with myself first, I would become so engulfed in the other person's suffering or need and make it my mission to ease their burden. However, it was also due to the fact that I had never seen healthy boundaries modeled in front of me as a child.

My parents found it difficult to draw a line separating who they were—and the suffering they were dealing with—from who their children were. As a result, they often transferred their stress, anxiety, and trauma onto us as kids, and because we didn't know better, we felt responsible for our parents' mental, physical, and emotional well-being. Furthermore, since the lines between parent and child were blurred, we didn't know which behaviors were acceptable and unacceptable. This meant that we accepted poor behaviors like disrespect, name-calling, gaslighting, and manipulation, because to us, this was how we related to our parents.

Under these circumstances, you can imagine just how difficult setting boundaries would be. Essentially, it would mean compromising the relationship my siblings and I had with our parents. After all, if we related to each other in an unhealthy way, setting boundaries would significantly change the dynamics of those relationships.

The inability to set boundaries caught up to me during my adolescent years. The dysfunctional parent-child relationship I had grown up with was repeating itself in other relationships too. Once again, the line separating myself and the other individual was non-existent, and this meant their frustrations or emotional needs were being transferred to me. It was an exhausting feeling knowing that the well-being of my friends and family rested on my shoulders, and that if I didn't rescue them from their troubles, I would be the one to blame.

My understanding of what boundaries were had been warped since childhood. I knew that I had to adjust how I perceived boundaries so that I could take care of myself better. While pursuing my psychology degree in college, I was exposed to what boundaries actually are. Instead of this high wall that keeps people at a distance, I learned that boundaries are a door that regulates access to my time, space, energy, and resources.

Imagine that you were given $1 million to build your dream home. You started by laying the foundation, then built two stories, and finally added all of the fixtures and trimmings to complete your home. But after the money had been spent and the day of moving in had arrived, you realized that there wasn't a front door. As beautiful as your home was, it was under a significant security risk because anyone could enter the house during the day or in the evening and violate your privacy.

Let's assume you managed to raise enough money to buy a door. Great. Now you at least have better security. However, the house door won't be open 24/7. In fact, there will be times when it's inappropriate to have guests because you aren't home or are enjoying quality time with your family. The door is therefore a form of communication to let others know when you are available and when you are unavailable.

Boundaries serve as a door into your life. It doesn't matter how strong your core values are or how much work you have put into your personal development—if you don't have healthy boundaries, your sense of peace and emotional safety is at risk. Anyone, whether it be a friend, family member, or colleague, can have unlimited access to your time, energy, resources, and space. But even if you have boundaries (you at least have a door), when they are weak or too flexible, people can often violate them and continue to act as they please and mistreat you.

If you would never live in a $1 million home without a front door, then why would you continue building relationships without any healthy boundaries? Your sense of emotional safety should be top priority, more than the need to please others. Just like you wouldn't leave your front door open 24/7, you also don't need to be available to others 24/7. It's okay, and even necessary, to be unavailable sometimes because there are urgent tasks, needs, and goals you have to work on before making time for others.

The Benefit of Setting Healthy Boundaries

Every human being has a public self and a private self. The public self is the aspect of an individual that others get to interact with. This may include their personality, behaviors, and attitudes. Generally speaking, the public self is shaped by the individual's environment, relationship expectations, social responsibility, and how others might see them. Thus, the public self is likely to change based on external factors.

However, there's also the private self, which is the aspect of an individual that is hidden from others. It consists of their internal values, beliefs, thoughts, and emotions. The private self is a lot harder to express openly than the public self because to do so requires a great deal of vulnerability. Plus, since the private self is not determined by others' standards, expressing this aspect of self can go against social, relationship, or environmental expectations.

Boundaries are set up to protect the private self, not necessarily the public self. They can teach you how to recognize your internal needs, beliefs, and desires, and then establish boundaries to honor these important parts of who you are. When you step out in public and interact with others, boundaries ensure that you don't reach a point where you compromise your private self. Thus, your social interactions, whether at work or at home, become less stressful and more fulfilling.

There are numerous benefits for setting boundaries. Below are some of the most compelling reasons why you need healthier boundaries:

- **Boundaries help to express who you are to others.** People can learn a lot from you by the type of boundaries you set in your life. They can learn about your likes and dislikes and behavior you deem as acceptable or unacceptable.
- **Boundaries help you draw lines between yourself and others.** Within intimate relationships, it's common to become enmeshed with those you love. You and the other person behave as though you're one entity instead of two unique human beings. Boundaries protect your individuality and make it easier to identify where your needs end and where the other person's start.
- **Boundaries help you decide how you wish to be treated by others.** It can be surprising for some adults to learn that they don't need to accept any kind of difference from others. By setting boundaries, they get to redefine their relationships and ensure that their interactions with others align with their core values.
- **Boundaries help you live a life that empowers you.** When you set boundaries, your needs take center stage in your life. This doesn't mean you become selfish, but instead live in such a way that improves your overall health and well-being.
- **Boundaries give you more control over your life.** You cannot control how others act toward you, but when you

set boundaries, you can control how you respond to bad treatment. Boundaries pull you out of a state of victimhood or people-pleasing and help you become a better version of yourself.

What I have found in my practice is that many people understand what boundaries are (at least at a basic level) and are familiar with the benefits of setting boundaries. However, what they often lack is the ability to tell the difference between weak, rigid, and healthy boundaries.

Weak vs Rigid vs Healthy Boundaries

We all have boundaries. If we didn't, we wouldn't have survived through some of the atrocities in our lives. Every human being has the capacity to stay away from perceived danger, avoid making bad choices, and find ways to alleviate suffering. Having these abilities is essentially what boundaries are all about. But having said that, not everybody has healthy boundaries.

Indeed, if you study the people around you or reflect on your own life, you'll realize that some boundaries don't offer as much protection or freedom as others. For example, you might get upset when you're mistreated and feel within you that a boundary has been crossed. However, due to having a weak boundary, you're unable to stand up for yourself and do something about it. On the opposite end of the spectrum, you might notice the mistreatment but, due to having a rigid boundary, you end up cutting off the individual from your life completely rather than having a discussion about the matter.

The point I'm trying to make here is that we shouldn't assume that just because we have boundaries that they're necessarily healthy. Weak boundaries look different from rigid boundaries, and rigid boundaries are not the same as healthy boundaries. To help you understand the difference, below are a few signs of weak, rigid, and healthy boundaries.

Signs of Weak Boundaries

Weak boundaries are generally those that don't offer sufficient protection. While you might be able to express your limitations, you may struggle to follow through with the appropriate action. Moreover, if you receive pushback, you're more willing to adjust your boundaries rather than hold the other person accountable. Here are a few signs you may have weak boundaries:

- **Your calendar is often fully booked because you agree to take on more tasks than you can manage.** At work or at home, you're typically the one who assumes the most responsibility because you're unable to set limits. You may find yourself saying yes to tasks or gatherings you don't want to commit to.
- **When you are disrespected, you would rather keep silent or air out your grievance with a third party.** Having to confront someone who has mistreated you is an uncomfortable experience, thus you try to avoid it as much as possible.
- **Being rejected by others is one of your greatest fears.** Even though you desire to be respected by those closest to you, being accepted by them is more important to you.

This means that you make a lot of personal sacrifices and compromises to stay in other people's good books rather than allow them to get to know who you truly are.

- **You internalize other people's thoughts and emotions.** It's difficult for you to separate your thoughts and emotions from another person's. For example, when someone is upset at you, you might assume you're responsible for making them feel that way instead of allowing them to take ownership of their emotions.

Signs of Rigid Boundaries

Rigid boundaries are on the opposite end of the spectrum. Instead of being too accommodating of others, you create boundaries that shut others out or severely punish them for boundary violations. Rigid boundaries tend to be a sign of anxious or avoidant attachment in relationships, where you prefer to create distance between yourself and others to protect yourself from getting hurt. While this distance makes you feel somewhat safe, it can be isolating and makes it harder to build healthy and mutually beneficial relationships. Below are a few signs that you may have rigid boundaries:

- **You are quick to block or cut people out of your life.** When you have been disrespected by others, you tend to take extreme measures to ensure the offense doesn't occur again. Rather than discuss the matter or allow the other person to apologize or explain themselves, you make an assumption that leads to blocking or cutting them out of your life.
- **You have strict rules about what you are willing to**

do and won't make any compromises. The good news is that you're able to articulate what you like and dislike, however you often find it difficult to bend your rules so that you can accommodate people who might think or desire something different from you.

- **It takes a lot for you to trust others in close relationships.** Most of your relationships remain shallow because you have a difficult time opening up to others. Due to this, you might attract people who are happy to talk about themselves constantly and won't bother getting to know you or ask how you're doing. These lopsided relationships might feel safe, but they are unfulfilling in the long run.

- **You are highly sensitive to criticism.** Since your guard is always up, you often feel personally attacked when others share thoughts or feelings that are unfavorable. In your head it sounds like they're ripping you apart, but this isn't the case. As a result of being sensitive to criticism, you may prefer to be around people who are agreeable rather than those who are likely to challenge you.

Signs of Healthy Boundaries

Ideally, we should all aim to set healthy boundaries. These normally fall somewhere between weak and rigid boundaries. You will know when you have set healthy boundaries because you won't feel vulnerable to disrespect, but won't be hypersensitive to it either. In other words, healthy boundaries allow you to set a standard for your life while recognizing that those around you have standards too, and in order to maintain healthy relationships, there must be mutual respect.

What differentiates healthy boundaries from weak boundaries is that you make clear and assertive limits. In contrast, what differentiates healthy boundaries from rigid boundaries is that they're flexible and can be adjusted when it's safe to do so. Therefore, what you end up with are boundaries that protect you from being mistreated by others, but also give you enough room to compromise in exceptional circumstances. Below are a few signs that you may have healthy boundaries:

- **You are able to separate your thoughts and emotions from others.** You are aware of your own physical, mental, and emotional needs and are able to express them whenever you need to. This means that you can easily identify thoughts and emotions that you disagree with or that might be projected onto you by others. For example, you can acknowledge that you aren't responsible for another person's emotional outburst.
- **You can articulate how you desire to be treated.** Since you're aware of what feels good and what doesn't, you can verbalize how you want to be treated. This might be as simple as saying no, or as elaborate as telling others what you need, what you are willing to accept (or not accept), and how they can show you support.
- **You are comfortable making choices that protect your interests.** There are times when you must make choices that don't benefit others, but protect your own interests. For example, you might decline an invitation to attend a social gathering because you're tired and would much rather have an early night. Even though you may feel guilty for not attending, you aren't worried about what others might think about your choice.

- **You are able to discuss your boundaries with others and hold them accountable.** The people closest to you are aware of your boundaries because you're open about discussing them. During conversations, or when a boundary has been crossed, you have the confidence to communicate your boundaries and request changed behavior. When your boundaries are repeatedly violated, you're also not afraid to enforce appropriate consequences.

Seven Types of Boundaries in Relationships

Healthy boundaries can be broken down into different categories to protect you in different aspects of your life. For example, you might desire to set limits when it comes to your personal space, privacy, or finances. Knowing what type of boundaries you need in your personal or work relationships will help you clearly communicate how you wish to be treated (as well as the consequences for boundary violations). Below are seven types of boundaries to consider:

Physical Boundaries

Your physical boundaries protect your need for privacy, personal space, and physical touch. It's always a good idea to let others know if their presence in your home, display of affection, or nosey behavior is making you feel uncomfortable. When communicating your physical boundaries, you might say:

- "I'm not in the mood for company tonight. Can we meet up tomorrow?"
- "I don't do hugs, but I can do a high five."

- "I'm not comfortable with you going through my phone."
- "May you please ask if I'm home before arriving at my house next time?"

Physical boundary violations will make you feel unsafe to be around a person. In extreme cases, these violations can lead to physical, sexual, or emotional abuse.

Emotional Boundaries

You have a range of emotions that deserve to be acknowledged and respected by those you're in relationships with. It isn't right for you to feel scared, judged, or embarrassed for expressing how you feel. Equally so, you shouldn't feel responsible for carrying another person's emotional baggage. Thus, emotional boundaries create clear limits when it comes to sharing feelings and resolving emotional situations. When communicating emotional boundaries, you might say:

- "When you yell at me during arguments, I feel disrespected."
- "I'm sorry that you're having a tough time. Since I'm not an expert, I can't speak much on the matter, but know that I'm here if you need someone to listen."
- "I'm not in the right frame of mind to have this discussion. Do you think we can have it another time?"
- "I prefer processing my feelings alone, but thank you for offering support. I truly appreciate it."

When your emotional boundaries are violated, you will feel judged, criticized, or misunderstood. If someone is emotionally dumping their frustrations onto you, it's possible to feel drained around that person or uncomfortable with the sensitive information you're being told. Other people, particularly those who are manipulative, might even make you feel guilty for expressing your emotional needs or take your kindness for granted.

Time Boundaries

How you decide to spend your time and who you decide to spend your time with is your personal choice. Time is a precious commodity because we can never earn it back; once it's been spent, it's gone. Therefore, if you value your time or perhaps live a busy lifestyle, you may want to set time boundaries with others so that you have more control over how you spend your time. Your time boundaries might sound like:

- "I won't be able to make it to the meeting tomorrow morning."
- "I only have 15 minutes to spare. What's up?"
- "I feel disrespected when you arrive to our appointments late. Next time I'll leave if you don't show up after 10 minutes of our agreed time."
- "I would be happy to assist you with this project. I charge an hourly rate of $50."

Time boundaries are violated when colleagues aren't punctual to meetings, when you aren't adequately compensated for your work, when friends cancel at the last minute on dates, or when a phone call with a friend drags on longer than you had agreed on.

Sexual Boundaries

Your sexual boundaries refer to your expectations when it comes to sexual intimacy, such as what type of sexual intimacy you're comfortable with, how often you prefer to engage in sex, your preferences when it comes to privacy, and so on. Sexual boundaries can sound like:

- "I'm not ready to be intimate with you at this stage."
- "I prefer it when you touch me like that."
- "I don't have sex without a condom."
- "I don't feel like having sex right now. Can we try later?"

It's extremely important for all parties to reach a mutual agreement on what kind of sex they would like to have. When consent is not given, or limits are not respected, a sexual boundary is violated.

Intellectual Boundaries

Similar to how you ought to feel safe sharing your feelings, you should also feel safe sharing your ideas and beliefs within a relationship. Since every human being is unique, there will be occasions where you enter into disagreements. This is natural and not something to feel bad about. In the heat of the moment, when you're engaging in a healthy debate or discussion with somebody, intellectual boundaries ensure that you're able to speak without fear of being shut down or dismissed. Your intellectual boundaries may sound like:

- "Let us agree to disagree."
- "You may not agree with me, but I don't tolerate name-calling."
- "I don't feel comfortable engaging in this topic any further."
- "I have the right to share my opinions too."

Intellectual boundaries are violated when your thoughts or beliefs are shunned or criticized. You might feel put down or invalidated. Remember that you can always end a conversation and walk away when you believe the discussion is unproductive or harmful.

Material Boundaries

Other great types of boundaries to have are material boundaries. These protect your material possessions, such as your money, home, car, or clothing from being exploited by others. It's important to be clear about what you're willing to share and what you prefer to keep to yourself. Moreover, you can communicate to others how you expect your material possessions to be treated. Your material boundaries may sound like:

- "If you want to use my car, may you please put gas inside it?"
- "I would love to help, but I only have $20 on me right now. Is this okay?"
- "Please ask for my permission before taking clothing out of my closet."
- "I'm happy to host the event at my house, but can you help me clean up afterward?"

When your material possessions are vandalized, stolen, or compromised by other people, your material boundaries are violated. You need to also be careful of those who use possessions like money to manipulate or control you.

Privacy Boundaries

Finally, privacy boundaries separate public and private information. When you share private information with someone, you might enforce certain rules about how they can safeguard your information. Privacy boundaries also govern who has access to your space, technological devices, social media accounts, work documents, passwords, cell number, and other materials that might contain sensitive information. Your privacy boundaries may sound like:

- "Please don't share what I'm about to tell you with anyone else."
- "I'm not comfortable being tagged on social media without my permission."
- "You don't have the right to access my emails."
- "Please don't mention my name or company in the article."

Privacy boundaries can also govern how much personal data you share with others or on social media. Make sure you read the privacy policies on your favorite apps or social networks to understand how your data is handled and protected.

Chapter Takeaways

- Boundaries regulate the amount of access people have to your time, energy, space, and resources.
- When you set boundaries in relationships, your needs, values, and expectations are considered during every interaction.
- Healthy boundaries are clear and specific about limits, but depending on the situation, they can be loosened to accommodate others.

2

Childhood Attachments and Boundaries

"The only people who get upset about you setting bound-aries are the ones who were benefiting from you having none."

— UNKNOWN

This chapter talks about:

- What makes a family 'dysfunctional' and how this dynamic can affect boundary-setting
- The three types of childhood attachment styles and how they manifest in adult relationships
- The effects of trauma on boundary-setting and what you can do to create a sense of safety

What Makes a Family Dysfunctional?

In an ideal world, each family is built on solid values, principles, and traditions that inform how family members relate to one another and protect the mental and emotional well-being of parents and children. The mutual trust and intimacy shared by both parents helps them identify themselves as the adults who are responsible for modeling healthy behaviors in front of their children.

Knowing that they are the adults and that there are certain experiences they cannot share with their children, such as their sexual intimacy or personal troubles, parents set boundaries to limit exposure to their private lives. However, a special bond is formed between parents and children that allows parents to protect, show affection, and teach their children the difference between acceptable and unacceptable behavior. Therefore, in the broader context, parents set boundaries for their children as a way to provide guidance, discipline, and teach them how to be responsible adults.

The unfortunate truth is that not every family is built this way. For instance, there are parents who are unable to identify themselves as the adults who are responsible for guiding their children. Instead, they might see themselves as being the ones who need to be taken care of. There are also parents who, due to their own childhood traumas and experiences, are unable to nurture their children or provide emotional validation—or they might be overly protective to the extent of smothering their children. Some single parents may even fail to keep sensitive information private and might depend on their children for emotional support.

These kinds of dynamics create what we call dysfunctional families. According to the APA, a dysfunctional family is one where relationships and communication between members is impaired, making it difficult for members to freely express themselves or feel close to each other (APA Dictionary of Psychology, 2022). One of the hallmarks of a dysfunctional family is the lack of clear and healthy boundaries.

In an ideal situation, healthy boundaries assist parents and children in defining their roles, setting expectations, and building trust. A lack of healthy boundaries blurs the roles that each family member plays and leads to issues like codependency, abuse, and emotional neglect. When parents are unable to model good behaviors or create structure for their children, it leaves the children feeling vulnerable. They might feel afraid to speak up for themselves, assert their own values or beliefs, or create their own identity apart from their parents.

Let's consider a common scenario of a lack of boundaries within a family: Imagine a child growing up with a parent who's a functioning alcoholic. When they aren't drinking, they're able to take on the role of adult in the relationship, become emotionally available for their child, and enforce healthy discipline. However, when they're intoxicated, the parent reverts to the role of being a child and cannot make logical decisions on behalf of the family.

The child grows up having to constantly switch between being a child (when their parent is sober) and being the adult in the relationship (when their parent is intoxicated). The child may have to take on adult responsibilities like cooking, cleaning, and paying bills, or even start working from an early age to cover for the negligence of their parent. Moreover, the child might also learn that it's unsafe to express their own needs or say no to their parent out of fear of receiving backlash or causing more conflict at home. Thus, the burden of taking care of the family falls on the child's shoulders, and they feel hopeless about doing anything about it.

You might be wondering how different this family dynamic would look if there were healthy boundaries. Well, first and foremost, if the family above had healthy boundaries, the parent would be more responsible regarding their lifestyle choices, particularly those that might violate the sense of security of their child. For example, consuming alcohol is not a bad thing, but when it starts to interfere with the ability to relate with others in a healthy way, there must be personal boundaries put in place. For example, the parent might restrict their alcohol consumption, especially when they're drinking around their child. This would ensure that their behavior is consistent and the child never has to step outside of their role.

Secondly, healthy boundaries between the parent and child could improve how both parties communicate with each other. The parent might speak freely about the kinds of behaviors they expect from their child, and the child might also feel comfortable expressing areas in their life where they need support. With words of affirmation and appropriate physical touch, both parent and child could affirm their love and appreciation for each other, and through this kind of relationship the family unit can be strengthened.

Being Close vs Being Enmeshed

In some families, dysfunction can be disguised as closeness. On the outside, the family appears to be affectionate, protective, and supportive of each family member, but if you look closer at the dynamic, you'll see that the boundaries between members have been blurred.

Families who are enmeshed don't encourage independence or autonomy. The parents who create this dynamic raise their children to depend on their instructions and put the needs and interests of the family above their own. In most cases, one or both parents have a desire to control the actions and future outcomes of their children by impressing their personal beliefs onto them.

When enmeshment occurs, boundaries become blurred. A controlling parent, for example, might violate the privacy of their child, make their child feel guilty for keeping certain information private, or encourage their child to go into career fields or pursue achievements that would reflect positively on the family. In other words, instead of developing a healthy sense of self, the child ends up becoming the image of what the family represents.

It's also difficult for a child raised in an enmeshed family to form relationships outside of their family. They might be discouraged from staying alone or spending too much time away from the family. When they do attempt to create their own separate life, they're often met with criticism or made to feel guilty, as though they were deserting their family. A parent with financial means may cut off their child financially for making decisions that aren't in the best interests of the family.

The difference between being close and being enmeshed is that a close family doesn't pressure its members to look within the family unit for satisfaction, support, and other emotional needs that could be found through external relationships. Children are free to express their individuality, cultivate meaningful relationships outside of the family, and make decisions about their own life. In contrast, with an enmeshed family, there isn't enough space given to each member to discover their sense of self and gain independence. Children often grow up with low self-esteem and being afraid to take risks or do anything that may upset their parents.

Since it's difficult to identify enmeshment when you're living in it, here are a few common signs of enmeshment in families:

- **Loyalty is overly emphasized.** People who aren't part of the family are often treated as "outsiders" and are not to be trusted. Parents might advise their children to stay away from certain social scenes or people, or to keep family secrets hidden from others.
- **Blurred family roles.** Parents might act more like their children's best friends rather than parental figures. This allows them to have more intimate access into their children's lives, but it also causes parents to overshare adult issues with their children.

- **Lack of privacy.** There's little concern for privacy within the family. For example, parents can arrive at their children's houses unannounced, call whatever time they want, or be overly opinionated about their children's personal relationships.
- **Feeling guilty when saying no.** Since solidifying a sense of self is frowned upon, children grow up having a difficult time expressing their needs and saying no. They may go along with their parents' wishes to avoid confrontation or tension.
- **Easily hurt when bids for affection are not received.** What reinforces enmeshment in families is the abundance of reassurance and affection that is given. This becomes somewhat addictive, and when a parent or child doesn't respond to bids for affection positively, the other family member may feel hurt or betrayed.

It's important to remember that enmeshed families also have a dysfunctional dynamic. Just because they're close doesn't mean that boundaries are respected and each family member's mental and emotional well-being is supported.

Attachment Styles in Adult Relationships

The nature of your family dynamic as a child affects how you relate with others in your adult relationships. One of the commonly cited theories that explains this is the attachment theory, discovered by psychiatrist John Bowlby and psychologist Mary Ainsworth (Robinson et al., 2021). The theory suggests that the bond you develop with your parents during childhood ends up becoming how you show up in other relationships and respond to intimacy.

There are four attachment styles that characterize the type of behaviors you might display in relationships, depending on your unique parent-child bond. By identifying which attachment style most represents your childhood, you can gain insight on the kinds of challenges you face in relationships, which can include the fear of setting boundaries or setting boundaries that are too loose or too rigid. Below is an outline of each attachment style and the type of boundary problems you may experience.

Secure Attachment Style

When you have a secure attachment style, you're able to open up to others and feel safe in intimate relationships. You have the ability to manage conflict well and take ownership of your mistakes or hold others accountable for theirs. Even though you're still learning about yourself, you're comfortable expressing your needs, thoughts, and feelings with others.

If you identify with this attachment style, it's likely that your parents were emotionally available for parenting when you were a child. For instance, they might have picked you up when you were crying, offered positive reinforcement, and created a safe home environment without being overly protective. This allowed you to grow up feeling supported and confident enough to make decisions, learn from your mistakes, and take healthy risks.

Due to your upbringing, you're aware of what healthy boundaries look like and you aren't afraid to enforce them when necessary. In general, you trust people and can be vulnerable when you feel safe in a relationship. However, your level of emotional intelligence can work against you if you aren't careful. For example, you might be overly concerned about the needs of others at the expense of your own well-being. Or since you're able to empathize with people, you might think it's your responsibility to fix them. Remember to respond to your needs first so you have the capacity to take care of others.

Anxious-Preoccupied Attachment Style

People with an anxious-preoccupied attachment style are typically needy in relationships. They tend to seek reassurance constantly, and may feel uncertain when they don't receive it. One of the main reasons for the constant seeking of reassurance is that they have a low self-esteem. They worry that they aren't good enough to be loved or take care of others.

If you identify with this attachment style, you were likely raised by hot and cold parents. One minute you were smothered with affection, and the next minute you were given the cold shoulder. This made you grow up feeling anxious about forming relationships with others and deep down fearing the possibility of being abandoned. In your adult relationships, you may crave intimacy with others, but your trust issues get in the way. When you do eventually open up to others, you tend to fixate on the relationship or become overly dependent on the other person.

The type of boundary issues you may experience involve space.

For you, being apart from friends and family for too long feels unbearable. When an intimate partner doesn't want to spend every minute of the day with you, you might feel offended. Moreover, you may find it difficult to truly express who you are with others because you fear being rejected. As a result, you might take on different personas depending on who you're around and have trouble saying no to others.

Avoidant-Dismissive Attachment Style

Think of people who display the avoidant-dismissive attachment style as being the polar opposite of those who identify as anxious-preoccupied. While the latter desires an extreme amount of closeness—and may even compromise their own needs to feel safe in a relationship—the former runs away or rejects any form of closeness. In fact, avoidant-dismissive people are so afraid of intimacy that they deliberately keep relationships on the surface.

If you identify with this attachment style, you were likely raised by parents who were emotionally unavailable or who abandoned you during childhood. Your needs for nurturing and affection were not met, and thus as an adult, you're uncomfortable with closeness. Part of your strategy to self-soothe was to build a wall around your emotions so that no one could hurt you. In adult relationships, you tend to be independent to a fault, not relying on others for assistance. You may even avoid people who are too emotional because you see them as being volatile and weak.

You're likely to have boundaries because these are what help you feel secure. However, unlike those with a secure attachment who cultivate healthy and flexible boundaries, your boundaries may lean toward being rigid. For example, you may be intolerant of other people's mistakes and take extreme measures to show your disapproval. Furthermore, due to your emotional unavailability, you may be responsible for violating other people's boundaries, such as keeping secrets, being promiscuous, or manipulating your way to getting out of trouble.

Disorganized Attachment Style

In most cases, people who develop disorganized attachment are survivors of childhood abuse and neglect. For them, the world is seen to be a dangerous place, and the only way to protect themselves is to emotionally shut down or withdraw from cultivating meaningful relationships. Think of this attachment style as the heightened form of avoidant-dismissive attachment.

If you've developed this attachment style, you've probably found it difficult to manage stressful situations like conflict, failure, and loss. Since you haven't learned the appropriate coping strategies, everyday life situations feel unsafe or overwhelming. Furthermore, without the necessary skills to build nurturing relationships, you're likely to repeat abusive patterns that were modeled in front of you as a child.

The type of boundary issues you might deal with revolve around your sense of safety. You might find it tough to ask others for what you need, and as a result are often unsatisfied with the quality of your relationships. Opening yourself to others may also be something you fear due to past negative experiences. Thus, as a way to hold onto others, you may seek to control or manipulate them. Even though you desire a sense of security in your relationships, you're also afraid of getting hurt again. What's even more saddening is that without the proper tools to process your trauma, you're vulnerable to substance abuse, obsession, and addiction.

How Does Trauma Affect Boundaries?

There are some adults who were exposed to childhood trauma and, as a result of their experiences, were unable to learn how to set healthy boundaries. We can define trauma as a painful event or experience that threatens your sense of physical and psychological safety. For instance, after going through a traumatic experience, you might be afraid of certain people or environments, or you can lose your ability to stand up for yourself.

Even if you weren't directly impacted by the trauma, meaning the painful event didn't affect you personally, you can still grow up with secondary trauma. For example, a child witnessing domestic violence can grow up feeling traumatized and being afraid of certain people or environments, even though they were not directly abused.

It's also important to realize that trauma is an umbrella term to describe various types of abuse, loss, and personal injury. When we speak of childhood trauma, we almost always mention the different kinds of abuse, but other forms of trauma may include:

- witnessing or being personally affected by a natural disaster
- experiencing emotional neglect
- being bullied or harassed
- facing financial insecurity
- witnessing a parent lose their source of income
- being raised by a mentally ill or addicted parent
- experiencing the death of a loved one
- having learning or behavioral difficulties
- being hospitalized with a serious illness

The effects of trauma can last a few months or could take years to resolve. Early therapeutic intervention can prevent PTSD and other trauma-related conditions. When medical assistance is not received, traumatic symptoms like flashbacks, nightmares, anxiety, avoidant behavior, emotional outbursts, or depressed moods can continue into adulthood.

One of the signs of unresolved trauma in adulthood is difficulty in setting healthy boundaries. Since you were never able to rebuild your shuttered belief system, process the grief, or learn how to create your own sense of safety, your boundaries are typically loose. This may attract manipulators who prey on your vulnerability and inflict even more emotional damage.

Below are a few signs that you may have loose boundaries as a result of living with trauma:

- **You are an oversharer.** People who are oversharers

tend to seek validation from others. This may be due to early childhood abandonment, where you felt like your parents' love needed to be earned. In adult relationships, oversharing could be your way of forcing a connection with others and trying to win over their love.

- **You often feel taken for granted.** You believe that others are constantly looking for ways to exploit you. This feeling may be due to your inability to say no or enforce consequences when boundaries have been violated. You somehow wish that people could read your mind and know when you have reached your limits.

- **You are attracted to people who don't respect your boundaries.** When you're living with unresolved trauma, it's common to recreate abusive relationships from the past. By doing this, you subconsciously hope to finally heal whatever part of you that was wounded as a child. Unfortunately, the cycle of abuse ends up repeating itself, and you're left with more emotional damage to process.

- **You are afraid to stand up for yourself.** Some types of trauma, particularly emotional abuse, can cause you to lose your sense of identity and independence. You may feel powerless to stand up for yourself when you have been mistreated, or fear the consequences of voicing your opinions.

- **You tend to feel anxious or stressed in social inter-actions.** When you're living with unresolved trauma, a part of you is still vulnerable to getting hurt. Social interactions can become terrifying because they present many opportunities for you to be triggered by someone or something. Moreover, since you don't have clear and firm boundaries, you fear being put in uncomfortable social situations.

Setting healthy boundaries can be the first step to healing from trauma. They can slowly help you regain structure, routine, and a sense of safety in your life, which can empower you to address other emotional issues. It's important for you to feel like you're in control of your time, energy, space, and resources, and to close the door for abusers and manipulators. Here are just a few ways you can get started on establishing healthy boundaries:

- **Be aware of your wants and needs.** It's common for trauma survivors to create a sense of safety by putting other people's needs first. However, this can cause them to neglect their own needs. Each day, take a five-minute break to check in with yourself and ask the question: "What do I need right now?"
- **Identify your tolerance levels.** Every person has a tolerance level. Finding yours can help you draw a boundary as soon as you feel uncomfortable or burned out. To figure out your tolerance level, think about a few relationship scenarios with friends and family that make you feel comfortable and some that make you uncomfortable.
- **Practice voicing your boundaries.** While it's good to write down your boundaries, eventually you'll need to communicate them to others rather than assume they know your limits. Looking into a mirror, express your boundaries in different ways, using different facial expressions, body language, and tone and pitch.
- **Get clear on your non-negotiables.** Part of healing

from trauma is giving yourself certainty that certain violations that occurred in the past will not happen again. For example, if you were emotionally abused in a past relationship, your non-negotiable might be name-calling. Think about some of the painful violations that threatened your sense of safety and create a list of non-negotiables. Create boundaries around these non-negotiables and ensure your loved ones are informed about them.

- **Don't be afraid of having different boundaries.** Your trauma impacted your life in a very unique way. As a result of overcoming painful experiences, you have a unique set of wants and needs. Realize that what is acceptable for someone else may not be acceptable for you, and that your friends and family may not always understand why you need a certain boundary put in place, but that doesn't mean you're wrong or that your boundary shouldn't exist.

Healing from childhood trauma is a journey all on its own, but having healthy boundaries put in place can make the journey feel a lot more comfortable. Essentially, when you heal from trauma, you're teaching your mind and body how to cultivate mutually beneficial and safe relationships again. Healthy boundaries can make it easier for you to articulate your thoughts and feelings around personal space, emotional needs, and expectations from others.

So far, you've learned the benefits of setting healthy boundaries, as well as the common reason behind a lack of boundaries in adult relationships. In the following chapter, you will discover what boundary violations look like and how to be assertive when holding others accountable.

Chapter Takeaways

- Growing up in a dysfunctional family can make it difficult to set and enforce healthy boundaries later in life. Instead, you're more likely to reenact the harmful relationship behaviors you learned—or saw as acceptable—when you were a child.
- Tight-knit families can create a nurturing and supportive environment for all members. However, when the closeness turns into enmeshment, boundaries become blurred and each member's rights and freedoms are stifled.
- Learning about your particular attachment style can help you identify specific boundary problems that you may be dealing with. For example, you might be overly needy of others and lower your standards in the process (anxious-preoccupied attachment) or you might be skeptical of others and find reasons to push them away with strict boundaries (avoidant-dismissive attachment).
- Depending on your childhood, you may be living with unresolved trauma. Setting healthy boundaries is the first step to regaining your sense of physical and psychological safety and learning how to communicate your needs.

3

What Boundary Violations Look Like

"The difference between successful people and really successful people is that really successful people say 'no' to almost everything."

— WARREN BUFFETT

This chapter talks about:

- what constitutes a boundary violation
- how to set and enforce appropriate consequences
- how to set boundaries with toxic friends and family

How to Tell When Your Boundaries Have Been Violated

Are you able to tell when someone has crossed the line with you? If so, how? Setting boundaries is winning half the battle. Enforcing these boundaries and making sure others are held accountable for boundary violations is the other half of the battle.

Celebrities are public figures whose boundaries are constantly violated. If it isn't one of their celebrity friends exposing their secrets, it's the paparazzi violating their personal space. While talking to *People* magazine in 2017, Oprah Winfrey accidentally announced her costar Mindy Kaling's pregnancy to the whole world. She told reporters that she was stunned when Kaling broke the news that she was five months pregnant.

Later on, Kaling admitted in a TV interview that Winfrey announced the news to the media. However, she didn't seem too bothered about it because of the status that Winfrey has. She said, "If anyone is going to announce big news about your private life, Oprah Winfrey is the person. You can't complain that much about it, and you also can't be like, 'Hey, Oprah, zip it,' because she's almost like a religious figure" (Price, 2017).

Imagine that it was one of her non-famous friends announcing a secret to the press—would that be considered a boundary violation?

Another celebrity that has experienced boundary violations is Jennifer Lawrence. Around 2014, the actress's nude photos were stolen from her personal device and leaked on the internet by some hacker who managed to get access to her iCloud account. But as if that wasn't enough of a violation, she has also been the subject of harassment by paparazzi.

In an interview, she expressed the emotional impact of being followed around by paparazzi all of the time: "I knew the paparazzi were going to be a reality in my life," she said, "but I didn't know that I would feel anxiety every time I open my front door, or that being chased by 10 men you don't know, or being surrounded, feels invasive and makes me feel scared and gets my adrenaline going every day" (Solove, 2014).

Just as Lawrence explained, having your boundary violated can make you feel anxious. It's similar to hearing a robber crack a window and forcefully enter your house. Boundaries are the imaginary lines you draw between yourself and others, thus when they're crossed you can feel deeply unsettled.

Due to the fact that no boundary is the same, boundary violations can look different for each individual. It's therefore up to each person to identify the criteria for a violation. Examples of internal boundary violations include:

- someone makes you feel worthless
- being yelled at or called names
- being told a lie or having a secret concealed from you
- receiving unsolicited advice
- feeling judged or criticized
- feeling controlled or manipulated

In contrast, external boundary violations may include:

- someone standing too close to you without your permission
- being touched without your consent
- having someone look through your belongings
- not being allowed to enjoy your privacy
- being pressured to smoke if you are a non-smoker

It's normally easier to tell when someone violates a physical boundary because they make you feel unsafe. For example, an unwanted touch can send shivers down your spine and cause you to feel vulnerable. Since these are not positive signs, you'll immediately recognize that a boundary has been violated.

However, you may have a difficult time deciphering when an emotional boundary has been violated because the signs are less obvious. For instance, if someone interrupts you while you're speaking, could this be a boundary violation or not? If your answer is "yes and no" then it proves just how tough it is to spot emotional boundary violations. Below are five signs that can help you identify emotional boundary violations when you're unsure:

- **You find ways of justifying someone's bad behavior.** While you're aware that what someone is doing or how they're treating you isn't right, you make up excuses for their behavior. The common excuse is "That's just who they are." If the person is battling with health issues, you may justify their behavior as a symptom of their condition.
- **You blame yourself for someone else's actions.** Instead of reacting appropriately to the offense by setting a boundary or issuing a consequence, you internalize the offense and see it as your fault. You might say to yourself, "If I didn't come home late, my husband wouldn't be insulting me."
- **You feel ashamed for calling the person out on their behavior.** You may feel like you're making a big deal out of nothing, or that you're causing more trouble in your relationship by communicating your boundaries or letting

39

someone know when they have violated a boundary. For example, you may feel ashamed of telling your partner that you need time alone because you don't want them to think you're checking out of the relationship.

- **You tend to second-guess your decisions.** After you have made up your mind about a boundary, you tend to backtrack on your decision when someone challenges it. For example, you tell your mother how excited you are to apply for a new job, and at first she seems happy for you. However, as the conversation continues, she challenges you about your readiness and competence for the position, which makes you second-guess the decision to apply for the job.

- **You feel uncomfortable around someone but don't know why.** You may feel uneasy when you're around someone who's violating an emotional boundary, but can't quite put your finger on what it is that makes you uneasy. Oftentimes, the person could be passive-aggressive or a master manipulator who covers their tracks and makes it difficult to hold them accountable.

- **Your opinions are disregarded.** When a mental or emotional boundary is violated, you tend to feel like your voice doesn't matter in the relationship. Whether you express your opinions or not, the other person will not acknowledge them. This can leave you feeling powerless to express your needs or hold the other person accountable for violating your boundaries.

Effective Ways to Respond to Boundary Violations

It isn't fair to expect others to understand or know how to adhere to your boundaries. Some boundary violations happen because those closest to you or those you work with aren't able to express the kind of respect, support, or consideration you need. However, that doesn't mean they should walk away scot-free after they have mistreated you.

The point here is that good-intentioned people can cross your boundaries too. When they do, it isn't always done to deliberately hurt you. But even when this is the case, good-intentioned people must be held accountable for violating your boundaries.

It's true that the people you love and respect the most are the hardest to confront about boundary violations. You might feel like doing so could jeopardize your relationship or make them treat you differently moving forward. However, think about the consequences of not holding them accountable. How much worse will your relationship get if a line isn't drawn? In general, the earlier you respond to a boundary violation, the better it will be for your relationship. This is because when both of you know where you stand with each other, you can deepen your level of trust and find the relationship mutually beneficial.

Depending on how safe you feel in the relationship, there are three ways you can approach boundary violators:

• When You Feel Safe in the Relationship

If you have already established healthy communication in the relationship and are comfortable expressing your thoughts and feelings, you can schedule time to sit down and speak to the boundary violator about your issue. If it's a violation that needs to be addressed urgently, like being cut off while you're speaking, then it's best to pull the person aside and express your concerns. However, if it's a violation that's deeply personal and might require some time to process, it can help to write down your feelings and think about what you want to say before approaching them.

When you have the conversation, remember to use "I" statements, such as "I feel" and "I need." Doing this helps the violator listen to you without feeling attacked or judged. Plus, when you use "I" you're showing the other person that you take full ownership of how you're feeling. For example, you might say "I feel disrespected when you cut me off while I'm speaking. Please be more mindful of your behavior next time."

• When Your Relationship Might Not Feel Safe

What challenges a relationship's sense of safety is the repetitive violation of boundaries. For instance, after you have made it known to a friend that you don't appreciate a certain behavior, they continue to do it anyway. What becomes obvious in these relationships is that the boundary violator is not willing to listen and respond to your needs. Perhaps they preferred it when you didn't have any boundaries, and now that you're setting boundaries, they're doing everything in their power to resist the change.

Once again, this resistance shouldn't stop you from addressing the boundary violations. If the violator isn't willing to speak to you about it, you can consider speaking to a therapist or trusted friend about your concerns. In some cases, a third party can advise you on ways to communicate better with the boundary violator, but if the violator is set on not respecting your boundaries, then any kind of intervention won't be successful. The bitter truth that's sometimes difficult to hear is that if somebody doesn't respect you, they won't respect your boundaries. Thus, this type of relationship will never feel safe because you aren't receiving the respect you deserve.

You may consider creating some distance so that they aren't close enough to hurt you. For example, you can ban someone who violates your personal space (like making a mess in your house or stealing your belongings, etc.) from coming to your house. Or you can stop giving out an invite to a friend who constantly has excuses for not attending your events or always arrives too late.

• When You Know Your Relationship Isn't Safe

Abusive relationships do not feel safe at all. The abuser has no sense of empathy for your needs and certainly won't respect your boundaries. Over the years, they have become comfortable disregarding your feelings, making you feel worthless, and turning the tables around when you confront them. Therefore, addressing boundary violations with abusers is no use. If you're not willing to stand for disrespect anymore, you can consider cutting off all communication with them and walking away from the relationship.

Of course, the more entangled your emotions are in the relationship, the harder it will be to leave. For example, if the violator is a boss at work you can look for a new job, but if the violator is a family member or romantic partner, leaving the relationship could feel wrong. Your support system will play a big role in helping you gather the strength to walk away from the relationship. If you don't have a support system, perhaps you can start creating one right now by finding a relatable and friendly therapist.

Addressing boundary violations with loved ones is about being clear on what respectful and healthy behavior looks like and trusting your gut instinct when deciding on the best ways to handle the situation. Some people may simply need to hear you articulating the boundary again in order for them to be on the same page. Others may not respect your boundaries no matter how many times you communicate them. Remember that your standards were never designed to accommodate the needs of your friends, family, and colleagues. They were put in place to protect your needs so that you feel safe in your relationships.

Of course, you can't force anyone to respect your boundaries, but you can enforce consequences when your boundaries are violated.

How to Create Effective Consequences for Boundary Violations

Believe it or not, many healthy boundaries that people set do not have consequences attached to them. This is because we operate under the assumption that those closest to us will honor our boundaries. However, as we have discovered, even good-intentioned people can violate boundaries.

Consequences are not a bad thing. They aren't a form of punishment that you issue whenever somebody disrespects you. All they're supposed to do is teach a lesson of cause and effect—with every action there's an equal reaction. For example, when a family member continues to enter your bedroom without permission, you might start locking your room when you're away. Your reaction is a consequence of their action. It's your way of showing the family member that entering your room without permission is unacceptable.

Contrary to popular belief, anger or the silent treatment are not consequences. They are emotional responses to a boundary violation. The reason why they can't serve as consequences is because they don't teach the violator a lesson of cause and effect. Using the same example as above, if you got angry each time your family member entered your bedroom without permission, would they learn a lesson? Your anger would be an inconvenience, not a reason for them to change their behavior. Therefore, strong emotions should not be used as consequences for broken boundaries.

The best consequences are not punitive, but corrective. Their objective is to teach the violator how to honor your space, time, energy, and resources. Each time they violate one of your boundaries, they get an opportunity to be reminded of what you expect. Thus, as you start creating consequences, remember that your aim is to teach a lesson in a respectful way and not to hurt or humiliate the violator.

In his book *Boundaries With Teens*, author and psychologist Dr. John Townsend presented five principles for setting effective consequences (Townsend, 2022). These principles can help you set consequences that teach a lesson and help violators understand your needs better. The five principles include:

1. Take Away the Desirable

Think of something the violator enjoys access to or depends on when it comes to you. Remove or limit access to that thing and place conditions. For example, if your friend gets into the habit of arriving late on your dates, you can cut down on the amount of times you meet up during the month or limit the amount of time you have to spend with them. You might say, "I only have an hour to spend with you. If you arrive late, then we'll have less time to catch up."

2. Let Natural Consequences Take Over

Since every cause has an effect, every bad behavior will have a negative consequence. What's great is the universe has a way of issuing consequences without you having to orchestrate anything. For example, if your romantic partner cheats on you, it could naturally be the end of the relationship. Or if your friend shares personal information about you, it will lead to distrust. The only thing natural consequences require from you is to not get involved by justifying the violator's bad behaviors.

3. Make the Consequence Significant

In order to be effective, a consequence must be significant to the other person. In other words, it should be strong enough to make them pause and reflect on their behaviors. They must be able to understand the impact of their actions and what they could possibly stand to lose if their actions don't change. A coworker who makes embarrassing comments about you in front of others might understand the impact of their behavior if you don't show any response—completely ignore what they have said and continue to engage with others. This would make enough of an impact for them to question their harmful actions.

4. Find the Most Lenient Consequence That Works

Once again, consequences are not supposed to feel like punishments, nor are they meant to cause harm to your relationships. If possible, you should create consequences that are lenient while appropriately matching the violation. For example, if you're disrespected by a colleague, giving them the silent treatment would be too lenient and may even lead to more disrespect. But limiting your communication to only work-related matters is an appropriate consequence that teaches them the value of respect. Remember that your goal is to correct bad behavior, not crucify someone for it.

5. Praise Positive Changes

After you have issued a consequence, keep your eyes open and watch out for changed behavior. It's important that the violator feels supported and loved throughout the process of submitting to your consequence. In most cases, having to go along with your consequences can make them feel ashamed or embarrassed, so be sensitive not to rub it in their face or make jokes showing you're in a superior position. For example, when you notice your partner is no longer raising their voice during arguments, mention how positive it makes you feel and thank them for respecting your communication boundary.

As you can see, consequences were never supposed to damage relationships; all they were meant to do is hold those you love accountable for their actions. Nevertheless, it's still possible that you're in relationships with people who undermine your consequences and refuse to be held accountable. For this reason, you might need to consider alternative options.

Setting Boundaries With Toxic People

Have you ever thought about what makes a relationship toxic? The truth is that any relationship that makes you feel worse rather than better about yourself can become toxic. While no relationship is perfect, and it's common to have disagreements with people, a relationship should never threaten your physical and psychological well-being.

Only you can determine if the bad traits or behaviors of a person outweighs their positive traits and behaviors. For example, one person may not have an issue with being called a curse word, while another person may feel demeaned when they're called a curse word. Nonetheless, when any behavior shifts from being innocent to being used as an attack, it can become toxic. Below are hidden signs that you might be involved in a toxic relationship:

- You invest more into the relationship than you're getting out of it.
- You constantly feel like your needs aren't being met.
- Your self-esteem has lowered since entering the relationship.
- You feel tired, anxious, or depressed after spending time with the individual.
- You notice yourself thinking or speaking negatively around the individual.
- Being around the individual brings out the worst side of you (E.g. you tend to gossip, judge others, or complain about life when you're with them.)
- You're afraid to express your true thoughts and feelings when you're around them.
- You spend a lot of time worrying if they're happy or being sensitive to their needs.

Toxic people can also come in all different shapes and sizes. What makes one person toxic might be different to what makes another person toxic. Learning about the different characteristics of toxic behavior can help you identify friends, family, and colleagues with toxic traits. Below are five types of toxic people:

- **The coworker who belittles you.** This person will make sarcastic remarks, implying that your thoughts or feelings are insignificant. They might make jokes at your expense or find ways to demean you in front of others. When confronting them about their behavior, they may say "I'm only kidding."
- **The parent with a bad temper.** Being around this person could make you feel on edge. You're never sure when they might erupt and have an emotional outburst. They're sensitive to criticism and don't like being questioned about their actions. When they feel under pressure, they'll lash out in rage.
- **The guilt-tripping partner.** This person feels safe when they have control in the relationship. One of the tactics they use to feel in control is to guilt-trip you. They often make you feel bad for not doing what they want you to do. When guilt-tripping doesn't work, they may accuse you of not being a loving or considerate partner.
- **The overreacting sibling.** When you attempt to confront this person about their boundary violations, they become overly emotional and make it difficult to hold them accountable. You might end up comforting them and forget the main purpose of your discussion. Another variation of this toxic trait is turning the tables around and making their bad behavior seem like it's your fault.
- **The overdependent friend.** This person is so passive to the extent that they rely on you to take care of them and make most of the decisions on their behalf. It can feel like you're caring for a small child who can't think for themselves, and this can be emotionally draining. When you can't be there for them, you may feel guilty or anxious

because you worry that something bad will happen to them.

Setting boundaries with a toxic person can be challenging because they have developed a habit of disregarding your needs and expectations in the relationship. However, that doesn't mean that they shouldn't face similar consequences as other good-intentioned boundary violators. When you have enforced consequences with a toxic person and they continue to violate your boundaries, there are few options available to you.

- **Decide whether the boundary is negotiable.** If the boundary being crossed isn't as important as some that are being respected, then you can consider making a compromise. However, remember that you're compromising with someone who isn't able to empathize with you, so being too lenient may come at the cost of your well-being. If the boundary repeatedly being crossed is non-negotiable, this could be a deal breaker in your relationship.
- **Get into the habit of writing down the violations.** Toxic people tend to twist the truth and use all sorts of manipulation to get you to doubt your own conception of reality. Write down every boundary violation, the consequence that was issued, and the response to your consequence. Having a record can help you when confronting the toxic person about their mistreatment, as well as when you're trying to weigh the pros and cons of the relationship.
- **Practice loving detachment.** When you lovingly detach from someone, you allow natural consequences to take

over. Instead of trying to fix them, you accept them for who they are and maintain a healthy distance. This could include blocking their number on your cell phone, moving out of the apartment you share, declining invites to meet up, and so on. The relationship may fizzle out on its own, or the person may return ready to respect your boundaries.

- **If the relationship has become too volatile to maintain, go no-contact.** When you go no-contact, your primary concern is your mental, emotional, and physical health. Sometimes, maintaining certain relationships can start to make you sick, lose motivation, or feel hopeless. Going no-contact gives you time to prioritize your well-being, address your own psychological issues, and reassess the value of the relationship.
- **Get support from a third party.** When you're in a toxic relationship, you can feel isolated from everyone else. It's important to reach out to people who can give you unbiased advice about your situation so you have the confidence to stand up for yourself. If you don't feel safe talking to friends and family, look for a friendly therapist who can support you on this journey.

When setting boundaries and holding toxic people accountable to them, remind yourself that you have a choice in the matter. Just because you have known someone for many years or have built a close bond with them doesn't mean that you need to put up with abusive or manipulative behavior.

Choosing to continue to work on a toxic relationship requires two willing participants. If you're the only person who's committed to working on the relationship, then you won't see the kind of positive change you seek. Plus, since it's impossible to force someone to respect your boundaries, getting a toxic person to respond to your needs and help you feel safe in the relationship won't work.

It's possible that you're not ready to distance yourself from the toxic person, and this decision is okay too. Remember, you have choices! Instead of going no-contact, you might decide to limit access or detach emotionally. Rely on your gut instinct to tell you which option is best for you at this particular time.

Chapter Takeaways

- It's easier to detect physical boundary violations, such as feeling uncomfortable when someone touches your body. However, emotional boundary violations may not be so easy to spot.
- The best way to figure out if your emotional boundaries have been violated is to check if you're making excuses for mistreatment, whether you feel guilty for confronting the person or if your opinions are disregarded.
- Communicating boundary violations will require a different approach depending on how safe you feel in the relationship. If you feel comfortable voicing your concerns, all it could take is a meaningful one-on-one conversation. But if you don't feel safe at all, you can consider turning to a mediator for support.
- When creating consequences, ensure that they match the offense and are designed to teach the violator a lesson rather than punish them for breaking your boundary. After submitting to the consequence, the violator is meant to

understand the impact of their actions and what they could lose if they don't correct their behavior.

- Toxic people may not respond well to consequences. Instead, they could use the confrontation as an opportunity to blame their behavior on your actions. You don't need to feel hopeless when setting boundaries with toxic people. Simply weigh your options and make a decision that protects your well-being. Once again, your support system will play a huge role in helping you safely walk away from a toxic relationship.

4

How to Communicate Boundaries Without Fear

"I set boundaries not to offend you but to respect myself."

— UNKNOWN

This chapter talks about:

- How to overcome the fear of what others might think of you
- How to define a healthy relationship according to your vision
- Phrases to use when communicating your boundaries assertively

The Fear of What Others Think

Have you ever been in a meeting and asked a question or shared your opinion, only for everybody present to stare at you like there was ketchup on your face? How did you feel at that moment?

We can't pretend that we aren't subconsciously hoping that the people around us like who we are. In fact, it's part of our human psychology to be concerned about what others might think about us. During the caveman days, our ancestors depended on groups, also known as tribes, in order to survive. Being part of a tribe was the security each individual needed to feel a sense of belonging.

Even though we don't operate in tribes anymore, there's still the natural human urge to form groups with others. We need a healthy dose of social validation to know that we're safe and valued. As we witnessed during the pandemic, being in complete isolation from others brought about anxiety and loneliness. Therefore, to some extent, we can't escape the need for relationships in our lives.

With all this said, when the need for relationships causes us to compromise on other physical, mental, and emotional needs, it becomes unhealthy. For example, when doing favors for others causes you to get behind on your work commitments, lose sleep, or put your goals on hold, then the cost becomes too high. Your generosity stops becoming a virtue, but rather a quality that makes you vulnerable to being taken for granted. When we are so focused on others that we make their thoughts and feelings more of a priority than our own, we risk satisfying other needs in our lives.

Caring about what other people think of us isn't bad, but living with the fear of what others might think can be harmful. For example, at work we might care about our reputation because it's important in building healthy work relationships. However, being afraid that our fellow coworkers don't like us can be a destructive thought. This is because it prevents us from taking necessary action and freely expressing who we are. We're always somewhat scared that we might step on someone's toes and make them upset.

The fear of what others might think can also make setting boundaries difficult. Since boundaries communicate our limits, we might be afraid that others may reject, ridicule, or judge us for drawing a separation between us and them. This often leads to loose boundaries that are too lenient and make us vulnerable to users and abusers.

It can be confusing to tell the difference between a healthy concern about how others perceive you and actually being afraid of what they might think (particularly if their perception is negative). Below are some of the common signs that you fear what others might think of you:

- When met with disapproval, you quickly change your stance and passively agree with the other person.
- If somebody comments about not liking something about you, you obsess about their comment until you start to see fault in yourself too.
- You prefer to let others make decisions for you, especially in a group setting where there may be a conflict of opinions.
- You are reluctant to express discomfort because you don't want to make the other person uncomfortable.

- You tend to beat yourself up when you make mistakes.
- You lose sleep over a disagreement with a friend or family member.
- You tend to apologize even when you're not in the wrong, just so you can clear the air.

If any of these signs have resonated with you, then it's a good idea to look for ways to not be so dependent on external validation. The following section will provide you with strategies on how to do it.

Strategies to Eliminate the Fear of What Others Think

Setting boundaries will continue to be a struggle until you overcome the fear of what others think. Recognizing that you're living with this issue is the first step. The second step involves practicing the following strategies:

- **Take People Off the Pedestal**

The first strategy is to remove anyone you have placed on a pedestal in your life. While it's normal to admire people, it's harmful to think that just because people are smart, beautiful, or successful that they're superior to you. Having skills, virtues, and talents doesn't make someone better than you, it simply means that they were able to cultivate their strengths. You have the same power to cultivate your strengths, thus there is nothing necessarily magical or supernatural about what they have done.

Start to see people for who they are, not who you have depicted them to be. Similar to you, every person you will encounter has strengths and weaknesses. They also have a complicated past and everyday work, health, and relationship struggles. Nobody you meet is perfect, nor can they achieve perfection. Therefore, when you observe people, have a sober evaluation of who they are and realize that you may have more in common than you think.

• Accept That Not Everybody Will Like You

If everyone had the same heart as your grandmother, perhaps they would think you were the best person in the world! But not everyone shares the same perspective as your grandmother. There are many reasons why some people won't like you—and most of them have nothing to do with you. In general, whether a person likes you or not has a lot to do with their formulated opinions (emphasis on 'their').

If you look at what informs a person's opinions, you'll find many factors that once again have little to do with you. For example, a person's opinion could be based on their upbringing, trauma, beliefs, emotions, desires, fears, and a whole bunch of other things. When a person rejects, criticizes, or judges you, all of these factors are triggered within them. Thus, it's impossible to connect with every person you meet or get them to understand your needs or where you're coming from.

• Remind Yourself That Hurt People Hurt People

It's unfair to expect someone who's dealing with emotional pain to treat you better than they treat themselves. Hurt people hurt people. This doesn't make their actions right or absolve them of any responsibility. However, it means that you can't expect them to empathize with you. Until they have gone through their healing process, they might always judge you negatively. Therefore, what they think of you isn't necessarily true, it's simply a reflection of their own pain.

• Recognize the Voice of the Inner Critic

There are times when you may think that someone dislikes you, but the truth is that you're projecting your own insecurities. The voice of the inner critic can sometimes sound like somebody else's thoughts and feelings, when in actuality they're your own thoughts and feelings. Be mindful of the internal dialogue you're having with yourself on a daily basis and how that might affect how you perceive yourself and others.

If you have a low self-esteem due to all of the past experiences you have endured, seek support from a therapist and slowly work toward having a positive self-perception. You can also consider cultivating deeper self-esteem by getting started with mirror work (refer to Chapter 5). When you can view yourself in a more positive light, it can become easier to tell the difference between your thoughts and what others believe about you.

• Hold Off on Judging Others

Another common reason that you might think others are judging you is because you're so used to judging others. In other words, you end up attracting the quality of thoughts you're constantly sending out. When you think negatively about others, you'll assume they're thinking negatively about you. However, if you were to think positively about others, you would assume they're thinking positively about you, too. The same applies to whom you call an enemy: An enemy is only an enemy because you have made them so. If you start to have a neutral or positive perception about them, they stop becoming an enemy. Thus, if you want to eliminate the fear of what others might think, practice thinking good thoughts about them and interpreting their actions in a positive way.

Craft Your Ideal Relationships

You may be able to set healthy boundaries in your current relationships, but if these relationships continue to feel unsafe, your boundaries may not work. In order to feel empowered in your relationships, safety is incredibly important, and moving forward, this characteristic might be something you look for in the relationships you form.

Healthy people who have good intentions will never put you down for setting boundaries. This is because they understand that relationships involve two unique people who have unique needs. Healthy people also understand the value of mutual respect and compromise. Instead of seeking to always get their way, they're considerate about your needs and feelings.

As you prepare to live a healthier lifestyle where your relationships feel safe and your needs are respected, it's worth thinking about the kind of relationships you desire. What do you want in a romantic partner, best friend, or boss? How do you want to feel when communicating with them? What kinds of values do you want to see shining forth? If you have grown up in a dysfunctional environment, you may not know what healthy relationships look or feel like. You may even think that you don't deserve to have relationships where you are honored, adored, and listened to.

I'm here to encourage you that healthy relationships exist, and that you deserve to have many of them in your life. You're not asking for too much when you say that you want to be around kind, honest, affectionate, generous, and friendly people. When it comes to romantic relationships, you're not asking for too much when you mention a list of qualities you need from your partner. In fact, relationship experts have found that there are qualities in a relationship that are more important than love, such as (Newsome, 2016):

- the ability to trust each other
- having a foundation of mutual respect
- feeling safe to express your thoughts and feelings
- having more happy experiences than hurtful experiences
- becoming good friends and leaning on each other
- maintaining your sense of self and having separate hobbies and interests
- showing commitment by actively making the relationship better
- regularly updating each other about your needs and boundaries

As you can see, love is never enough when it comes to building healthy relationships. Take a moment and think about your existing relationships in different areas of your life. Reflect on the current state of these relationships and what qualities are missing in order for you to feel satisfied. Write down a list of these qualities—you'll need them when you complete your relationship vision statement.

How to Create a Relationship Vision Statement

The concept of a relationship vision statement may seem strange, however, just like companies establish a vision statement, so can you when crafting your ideal relationships.

A relationship vision statement gives you the opportunity to think about the quality of interactions you desire based on your needs, beliefs, values, and past experiences. Unless the people you're in relationships with have a similar vision, you'll often have disagreements or communication issues.

Starting off new relationships with a vision can set you up to succeed. But this doesn't mean that your existing relationships can't benefit from a vision either. Of course, both you and the other individual must agree that your relationship needs a fresh start and work together to form a new vision. If it's only you who desires a fresh start, this exercise won't be useful.

Below are the steps on how you can create a relationship vision statement together with the person you're in a relationship with:

Step 1: Write Down 'We' Statements
On separate pieces of paper, write down statements about

the kind of relationship you want. Start each statement with the word 'we,' like "We enjoy spending quality time together." Ensure that each statement is written in the present tense, as though it's how your relationship is operating right now. Write down 5–10 statements, and when you're done, read them aloud to each other.

Step 2: Discuss and Consolidate Your Lists

Take turns discussing each statement in more depth to truly understand the expectation. You're welcome to raise questions and challenge the expectations in a respectful way. For example, you might say, "I hear that you'd like us to spend more time together, but what happens when I'm busy throughout the week?" Remember, challenging isn't the same as judging. You challenge by validating what the other person is saying and sharing your ideas, thoughts, or concerns to trigger a deeper conversation and compromise.

After you have discussed each statement, decide on which vision statements you agree on and would like to work on together. Not every statement on your list or theirs will make the final list. This is okay. The final list should only consist of vision statements that hold true and feel meaningful for both of you.

Step 3: Hold Each Other Accountable

Your final list should be treated as a working document, meaning that you're both constantly editing, adding, and removing statements according to your relationship's needs. Make copies of the list so that you can both access it regularly and hold yourselves and each other accountable. For example, if your friend raises their voice at you during a conversation, you can remind them of your vision statement that states "We will speak to each other with respect." This is how you can ensure your relationship reflects ideals that both of you share.

If you need inspiration on what relationship vision statements look like, below are a few examples to consider:

- We are free to share any thought or feeling without being judged.
- We spend at least one weekend in the month together.
- We speak highly of each other to friends and family.
- We avoid making jokes about each other's feelings.
- We compliment each other often.
- We tell each other the truth even if it's painful.
- We explore new activities together.
- We have sex at least once a week.
- We respect each other's need for privacy.
- We support each other's goals.

Communicating Boundaries Assertively

Getting over the hurdle of what others think will give you the necessary confidence to ask for what you need. This doesn't mean that your boundaries will always be well received, but it does mean that you'll be able to draw limits with others. A great communication skill that will improve how you articulate boundaries is assertiveness.

To be assertive is to stand up for yourself and what you believe in. Assertive communication, therefore, is a style of communication where you make confident statements while showing respect to others. It shouldn't be confused with arrogance, since an arrogant speaker is self-absorbed and will not listen or empathize with the other person.

Assertive communication is also not defensive, nor is it aggressive. You don't need to raise your voice or intimidate others to get them to listen. In fact, aggressive communication is more likely to cause the other person to shut down or walk away, which prevents you from getting what you need.

Assertiveness is important when communicating boundaries because it sends a clear and direct message. Unlike passive communication, where the listener is confused about what you're actually saying, assertive communication gets down to the nitty-gritties and states boundaries boldly. For example, instead of saying to a friend, "Oh, so you're ignoring me now?" which is a question that's hiding a deeper meaning, you can plainly say, "I don't feel seen or loved when you give me the silent treatment. If you're not prepared to talk, I'll leave."

What's the difference between these two statements? The first one is indirect and somewhat sarcastic. It's likely to aggravate your friend rather than allow them to see how their behavior is impacting you. The second statement focuses on your experience rather than theirs, and sets a boundary followed by a consequence.

Now practice saying both statements to yourself and notice the difference in tone. The first statement doesn't allow you to convey as much clarity and confidence as the second one. And this is why assertive communication will always work when communicating boundaries.

Constructing assertive statements isn't as difficult as it seems. There's a simple formula that you can follow whenever you desire to convey messages assertively:

- **Think about what you want to say and write it down.** Don't skip this step because it'll help you map out your thoughts and ensure you're being as clear as possible. Sometimes when you have a million thoughts running through your mind, it becomes tough to know exactly what boundary has been violated and the appropriate consequence to issue.
- **Tune into your feelings.** Assertive communication places the spotlight on your experiences. For example, instead of saying "You make me feel," you would say "I feel." Check in with yourself and figure out what emotions were triggered when your boundary was violated. Write these emotions down on paper too, starting with "I feel" or "I felt."
- **Mentally prepare yourself to enforce the consequence.** After demonstrating confidence in communicating your boundary, you must be willing to follow through with the consequence if the other person isn't willing to listen. Think about what you'll do if the other person is uncooperative. Have at least three different options that you can revert to at that very moment.

So far, you understand what assertive communication is and how to construct assertive statements. Now we'll get a little bit more specific and look at five elements that your statements need in order to qualify as assertive.

• Clearly Describe the Transgression/Behavior

It's important for the other person to understand what they might have done to offend you. Remember, even good-intentioned people can violate boundaries, so we can't assume that everyone who violates our boundaries means any harm. By explaining what has happened, you give them an opportunity to reflect on their behavior and see where they might have gone wrong.

Here's an example of describing the transgression/behavior:

"When you interrupt me while I'm speaking..."

• Be Honest About the Emotional Impact

The next component is displaying vulnerability by sharing your feelings. This will probably feel awkward if you aren't used to expressing your emotions, but it explains why the boundary violation means so much to you. If the relationship doesn't feel psychologically safe, you may not feel comfortable opening up about your emotions. This is okay, and you shouldn't feel guilty for not trusting another person with your emotions. Simply remove this component from your statement.

Here's an example of conveying the emotional impact:

"I feel frustrated."

- **Share Your Thoughts**

It's common for a boundary violation to make you draw assumptions or perceive the violator in a certain way. Once again, it's important for the other person to know what thoughts are running through your mind when they violate your boundaries. This gives them an opportunity to step inside your shoes and imagine what you're experiencing. When sharing your thoughts, be respectful and considerate of their emotions too. While it's good to get everything off your chest, it's never good to make another person feel small, insulted, or ashamed.

Here's an example of sharing your thoughts:

> *"It makes me think that you don't care about my opinions."*

- **Suggest an Alternative Behavior**

The goal of communicating boundaries isn't to punish the other person, but to teach them about how they can respond to your needs better. Therefore, a crucial component of your statement is the alternative behavior. Instead of their current behavior, think about how they can act differently (within reason, of course). The alternative behavior must be realistic and simple enough for the other person to follow.

Here's an example of suggesting an alternative behavior:

> *"I would appreciate it if you waited for me to complete my train of thought before you speak."*

• **Clearly Define the Consequences**

Lastly, end your assertive statement by defining the consequences. In other words, if the other person doesn't make the effort to follow the alternative behavior, what will you do in response? Remember to choose a consequence that matches the violation and is effective while also being a teachable moment.

Here's an example of a definitive consequence:

> *"If you continue interrupting me while I speak, I'll disengage from the conversation."*

Now, let's combine all five components to see how communicating boundaries assertively looks and sounds like:

> *"When you interrupt me while I'm speaking (1), I feel frustrated (2). It makes me think that you don't care about my opinions (3). I would appreciate it if you waited for me to complete my train of thought before you speak (4). If you continue interrupting me while I speak, I'll disengage from the conversation (5)."*

Practice saying this paragraph in the mirror. Repeat it over and over again until you feel a sense of confidence take over your body. This is the kind of confidence you need when approaching someone who has violated your boundary.

Phrases to Help You Communicate Boldly

Communicating boundaries won't come naturally at the beginning, but with much practice, you'll learn how to articulate yourself better. To end off the chapter, I'll present to you phrases that can become your template when communicating boundaries.

To start off with, here are sentence openers that you can use to initiate a conversation about your boundaries:

- "I would like to bring something to your attention."
- "May I please make a request from you?"
- "I would like to revisit the incident that took place yesterday."
- "I have taken the time to think about your request."
- "Is this a good time for us to have a heartfelt conversation?"

There are also specific phrases that you can use when setting certain kinds of boundaries. For example, you can use the following phrases when disagreeing with someone in a respectful way:

- "I disagree with your approach to this situation."
- "I'm not willing to change my mind about this matter."
- "I hear what you're saying. However, that hasn't been my experience."
- "Your ideas are fascinating. However, I'm not sure how they would work in practice."
- "Let's agree to disagree on this subject."

There will be times when you'll need to make it clear that the answer is a firm 'no.' Here are a few phrases to help you state your position confidently:

- "I don't have the time to take on more projects."
- "I know my original response was yes, but after looking at my schedule, I can't commit to any more tasks."
- "I can't answer your call right now. Please send a text."
- "I would be happy to help you, but my hourly rate is $100."
- "I can't see you this weekend. Let's reschedule for another time."

In certain situations, you'll be put on the spot and forced to set a boundary at that moment. An example would be someone asking you a question that you're unprepared to answer. Here are some phrases that can help you set boundaries right there and then:

- "I'm uncomfortable answering that question."
- "Give me some time to have a look through my emails and I'll get back to you."
- "I'm not in the position to share that information with you."
- "I'm not in a good place to have this conversation right now."
- "I'm not an expert on that topic, but I'll find someone who is."

Every now and again, you'll encounter people who are negative and seek to bring you down. They may be your friends, family, customers, or strangers you meet in public. Here are some of the ways you can set boundaries and protect your mental and emotional well-being:

- "Please excuse me while I take five minutes to recollect myself."
- "I'm feeling overwhelmed by this conversation. I would like us to change topics and come back to this subject later."
- "What you have shared with me is a lot to take in. Please give me a few days to process this information and I'll get back to you."
- "I feel misunderstood and I don't think we'll get very far with this topic. Let's agree to disagree."
- "I don't appreciate being spoken to like that. You can disagree with me, but insulting me is unacceptable."
- "I would like us to find a middle ground, but if you aren't prepared to compromise, I'm willing to walk away."

Sometimes, you'll want to convey the emotional impact that a boundary violation has on you. Here are some of the ways you can describe your emotional experience:

- "I feel afraid to be honest with you."
- "I don't feel like my needs are being considered."
- "I feel shut out when you emotionally withdraw from me."
- "I feel undermined when you tease me in front of our friends."
- "I feel betrayed when you share my secrets with your family members."
- "I don't feel comfortable opening up to you about that situation right now."

Finally, there will be times when good-intentioned people

give you unsolicited advice. Instead of putting them down, you can set a clear boundary and redirect the conversation to something else. Here are a few phrases to help you:

- "I think we're getting distracted. Let's focus on the task at hand."
- "I value your friendship, but this is a family matter."
- "Thank you for those encouraging words. I'll go home and think about it."
- "That may have been the case in your situation, but my situation is different."
- "Let me talk to my partner first and then I'll get back to you."
- "I understand that you have more experience, but allow me to do it my way."

Chapter Takeaways

- Caring about what others think of you isn't necessarily a bad thing. However, when you become fearful of criticism or judgment, it can hold you back from making decisions that could improve your quality of life.
- Realize that not everybody will like you or have enough empathy to accept you as you are. Their dislike of you has more to do with their personal experiences, biases, and assumptions than who you are as a person.
- You can protect yourself from one-sided or unsupportive relationships by creating relationship vision statements with your friends and family and holding each other accountable to that shared vision.
- When communicating boundaries, assertiveness is key.

It gives you the confidence to stand up for yourself while being mindful of others. The five components that make boundary statements assertive are: describing the transgression, describing the emotional impact, sharing your thoughts, suggesting an alternative behavior, and defining the consequence.

5

What Self-Love Has to Do With It

"Loving yourself does not mean being self-absorbed or narcissistic, or disregarding others. Rather it means welcoming yourself as the most honored guest in your own heart, a guest worthy of respect, a lovable companion."

— MARGO ANAND

This chapter talks about:

- The emotional impact of not being shown love as a child
- How to identify old relationship patterns so you can stop attracting toxic people
- The true meaning of self-love and steps on how to get started with mirror work

Robbed of the Affection You Needed

Love is an emotion that's essential for your survival. It isn't optional, nor is it a privilege that only some people get. When you're robbed of love, you become physically, mentally, and emotionally sick. The lack of love, especially in the lives of children, is serious enough to cause trauma.

Love is more than hugs and kisses. It's about feeling safe and accepted. Think back to some of your earliest childhood memories and connect to your emotional experiences. Reflect on how your parents made you feel in their presence and absence, or how you felt living in that household environment. If what you felt back then was fear, confusion, stress, or unworthiness, then it means your parent-child relationship or the household environment lacked love.

If you want to dig deeper, you can even think about nonverbal cues that your parents showed that signaled being emotionally unavailable. A few of these might have been avoiding eye contact when you spoke, being short-tempered, failing to soothe you when you were distressed, invalidating your feelings, and so on.

The lack of love in childhood may have affected you in several ways, but one of them was in how you built your sense of self; who you believe you are and what you believe you deserve. Being raised by emotionally unavailable parents meant that you weren't able to see yourself correctly. You interpreted the coldness or neglect as a consequence for being a certain way. Instead of viewing your parents' behaviors as a sign of their own dysfunction or mental health issues, you internalized the mistreatment and saw it as a reflection of who you are.

An example of this would be a daughter who was raised by a narcissistic mother, but is too young to see her mother's self-absorbed and controlling behavior as a sign of her own psychological state of mind. She internalizes her mother's daily criticism and gaslighting as a sign that she needs to change something about herself. "Perhaps if I just shut up and agreed to what mom says," she thinks, "then she'll be pleased with me." Desperate to receive her mother's unconditional love, she internalizes the criticism and seeks to correct "flaws" in her own character. Of course, the worse her mother's behavior gets, the more flaws she believes need to be corrected in herself.

Maybe you have a similar experience of questioning your character as a result of internalizing your parents' suffering. Due to being young and not having a sense of boundaries, you internalized the negative energy and dysfunction in your environment and developed a warped sense of self. You may have even concluded that you're unlovable or that you don't like affection, only because you were robbed of unconditional love.

You might be wondering what all of this has to do with setting boundaries. The lack of love during childhood creates patterns later on in life. These patterns can manifest in different ways, although they all resemble the dysfunctional parent-child relationship. For instance, not being shown love as a child can make you desperate for love as an adult, which often means compromising your own standards just to please others. You're so desperate for others to validate you to the extent that their thoughts and opinions about you matter more than what you believe about yourself.

Another pattern that could manifest is pushing people away because you don't trust that they can protect you and give you the kind of love you need. You may even adopt the belief that love is dangerous (if you were abused by someone you trusted) or that love is painful (if you were betrayed). These beliefs cause you to place barriers between yourself and others, making it extremely difficult to connect or build intimacy.

These patterns continue to unfold in your adult relationships until you recognize them and make different choices. One of the first choices you will need to make is to stop looking at love from a negative perspective and start embracing the idea that healthy love exists, and you deserve to experience it!

How to Stop Attracting Toxic People

A quote that I read a while back said, "You stop attracting certain people when you heal the part of you that once needed them." (Tygielski, 2017) It may sound strange to think that a part of you is drawn to people who disrespect your boundaries or prove to be unreliable or emotionally unavailable after knowing them for some time. However, if you understand the fact that your adult relationships follow patterns you learned from childhood, it becomes a lot easier to accept why you're constantly attracting one toxic person after the next.

Another uncomfortable truth to hear is that due to not receiving sufficient nurturing and affection as a child, opening yourself up to healthy and loving relationships feels terrifying. In other words, having someone treat you with respect, be attuned to your needs, and respect your boundaries can make you suspicious, and you might unintentionally find ways of sabotaging that healthy relationship.

Responding negatively to love is a sign of childhood trauma that must be addressed before you can cultivate healthy relationships. This behavior prevents you from making genuine connections with good-intentioned people. In fact, when a stable and secure person notices how detached you are from your feelings or how defensive you get when they attempt to get close, they will often walk away from the relationship. A toxic person, on the other hand, will notice the same negative behaviors and feel safe in your company because they respond to love in the same unhealthy way.

To process and overcome your negative views about love, it's important to understand what causes you to react to love in that manner. Below are the three main reasons you may find it difficult to accept genuine love:

- **Being genuinely loved makes you feel anxious because it threatens your defense mechanisms.** To protect yourself from emotional distress, you learned defense mechanisms, like pulling away, acting indifferent, or getting angry. Healthy love challenges these defense mechanisms and leaves you feeling vulnerable.
- **Being genuinely loved triggers feelings of disappointment from the past.** When someone comes into your

life and desires to love you without asking for anything in return, this can bring up pain from the past, particularly relationships where you felt like you had to earn the other person's love. You may feel afraid of experiencing the same disappointment all over again.

- **Being genuinely loved causes you to question who you are.** Since your sense of self was built on internalized negative beliefs and experiences, being in a loving relationship can feel confusing because it challenges who you grew up thinking you were. All of a sudden, you're forced to question your feelings of inadequacy and other insecurities that aren't being mirrored back to you in this healthy relationship.

Since you're a creature of habit like any other human being and rely on learned patterns, defenses, and habits to protect yourself, you're more likely to recreate the relationship you had with your parents growing up in your adult relationships. Even when you have the opportunity to meet wonderful people who are willing to respect your boundaries, you will subconsciously seek to maintain a sense of pseudo-safety by sabotaging the healthy relationship. For example, if you sense that someone admires you, it might cause you to create distance or find a way to cause conflict. Or you might find a way to provoke the other person so that they recreate the same dynamic you experienced with your parents.

What's most interesting is that you may not even realize that you're pushing good people away and attracting toxic people toward you. Remember, all of this tends to happen on a subconscious level. To end the cycle of dysfunctional relationships and start cultivating healthy relationships, you'll need to learn how to identify your self-sabotaging behaviors.

Recognize the Old Relationship Patterns

Have you ever wondered why someone would treat two people differently? To the first person they're polite and agreeable, but to the second person they're obnoxious and self-centered. It isn't because they have two different personalities, but instead that each person places a different demand on them.

When you don't have any boundaries to protect your physical, mental, and emotional well-being, you give those around you the license to treat you however they want to. Instead of placing a demand on them, like being very clear on your intolerance of disrespect, you accept whatever treatment given. Someone else who might have more solid boundaries might correct people whenever they step out of line, which influences how those around them act.

If you're tired of being surrounded by negative people, manipulators, or those who are emotionally unavailable, it's time to look at yourself in the mirror and ask a sobering question: *What demands have I placed on those around me?* If you haven't placed any demands, don't be surprised when your boundaries are frequently violated. The truth about toxic people is that they can only get away with as much as you allow them to. When you decide to stop participating in their dysfunctional patterns, they won't have an opportunity to take advantage of you.

The kind of treatment you were accustomed to receiving as a child is the kind of treatment you expect—and sometimes seek—in others. This creates a toxic cycle where your adult relationships reinforce behaviors that were acceptable or normal growing up. Earlier on, in Chapter 2, we discussed the four attachment styles. If you're still unclear about your attachment style, please go over that chapter again. Learning your attachment style gives you insight on patterns that you must break in order to stop sabotaging yourself in relationships.

It's also crucial to be honest with yourself during this time about your ideas of love. Reflect on what your relationship with your parents taught you about love. If you didn't have healthy love modeled in front of you as a child, you'll tend to have a negative or limited understanding of love. Breaking old relationship patterns involves challenging these ideas about love by holding them loosely and being open to change your mind. You can undo these patterns by simply acknowledging that unconditional love isn't supposed to hurt.

A scripture in the Holy Bible describes what unconditional love is supposed to look and feel like (*New International Version*, 2011/1984, 1 Corinthians 13:4-7):

> Love is patient, love is kind. It does not envy, it does not boast, it is not proud. It does not dishonor others, it is not self-seeking, it is not easily angered, it keeps no record of wrongs. Love does not delight in evil but rejoices with the truth. It always protects, always trusts, always hopes, always perseveres.

What Is Self-Love?

Learning how to love yourself when you weren't shown affection or given positive reinforcement as a child can be really difficult. It requires more than just spoiling yourself with new clothes or gadgets, going to the gym, or wearing makeup. Self-love is about making up for the emotional needs you hadn't received as a child and reparenting yourself. In other words, making it your responsibility to care for your physical, mental, and emotional well-being.

Self-love can be defined as showing up for yourself. You can do this in three different ways: forgiving, accepting, and respecting who you are. Let's look at each of these components in more detail.

- **Self-Forgiveness: Hold Yourself Accountable for Self-Inflicted Pain**

When thinking about forgiveness, you might think about forgiving others for the hurt they have caused you. But how often do you think about the hurt you allowed against yourself? What about the many times you betrayed yourself by accepting the bare minimum from people, allowing others to walk all over you, or making decisions that sabotaged your sense of safety?

The reason self-forgiveness is crucial to cultivating self-love is because before you can love yourself, you have to be honest about the role you have played in your own suffering. This doesn't excuse wrongdoers for what they have done to hurt you, but it also doesn't allow you to walk away scot-free. You must be able to sit down with yourself and take responsibility for pain that was self-inflicted. Setting loose boundaries, for example, is self-inflicted pain because when you fail to stand up for yourself, you can't hold others accountable for their mistreatment.

Take a moment right now and think about some of the ways you have inflicted pain upon yourself by not protecting your physical, mental, and emotional well-being as well as you should have. Please note that reflecting on your own shortcomings is not a form of judgment or thinking poorly of yourself. Instead, it's a way for you to confront injustices that you have permitted in your life with honesty and transparency. You are not a bad person for having these shortcomings, and they certainly don't define who you are. However, if you desire to deepen self-love, you should be able to have tough conversations with yourself about unacceptable behaviors you exhibit that are unloving.

• Acceptance: Be Content With Who You Are

The moment you come to terms with your own acts of deception, you can move forward and learn to accept yourself as you are. Acceptance is an important part of cultivating self-love because you make peace with the person you see in the mirror. Yes, that individual is flawed and may even be holding on to a lot of pain from the past, but take a closer look at them and you'll see a survivor.

Every human being has a story, and if you were to learn about their story, you would understand something about life: Bad things happen to good people too. Just because your life story didn't unfold like a fairytale doesn't mean you were destined to live an unfulfilling life. Certainly, there are many past events that you wish didn't happen or that you wish you could change, but even those painful events played a role in shaping who you are today.

Accepting who you are is about putting down your mental weapons and ending the inner war that has continued for so many years. Instead of finding fault in yourself, you embrace your weaknesses and admit to your own dysfunctional behaviors. You recognize that you have limitations and sometimes these limitations get in your way. This level of honesty with yourself makes it possible to feel comfortable in your own skin. When you're comfortable in your own skin, you can start to appreciate your life and become more sympathetic to your own needs.

• Respect: Treat Yourself Like a VIP

When you love something, like a gadget, piece of clothing, or jewelry, you're extremely careful about how you take care of it. You might place it in an isolated area, so that no one else has access to it, or put terms and conditions about how others can use it. The same applies when you love another person, like a close friend or sibling. You're protective over them and care deeply about their well-being. If they're upset, you get upset too because you have a lot of compassion for them.

Self-love is compassion and consideration directed inwards.

Because you think highly of yourself, you're protective about your mental and emotional well-being. When you detect discomfort (whether physical or emotional), you respond immediately and restore your sense of wholeness. The reason you think highly of yourself and go to such great lengths to show yourself compassion is because you respect the person that you are.

Self-respect is the confidence you have in yourself that causes you to behave with dignity. Just like a precious piece of jewelry, you limit the access people have to you, especially to your private life. Moreover, you set standards regarding how others treat you and hold them accountable whenever they don't meet your standards. You don't have to be rich, classy, or famous to treat yourself with self-respect. All you need to do is recognize that you're worthy of love and good treatment from yourself and others.

One of the barriers that prevent you from deepening the love you have for yourself is the fear of what others might think. In this context, you may be afraid that others will think you're being selfish for treating yourself like a VIP, setting healthy boundaries, and honoring your needs. Or maybe your fear stems from growing up in a family where self-love was seen as indulgent, whereas self-sacrifice was seen as noble. Whatever the case may be, it's important to challenge the idea that self-love is wrong.

If you remember the last time you were on a plane, the air host or hostess gave you and other passengers flight safety precautions. One of those precautions had to do with the loss of cabin pressure. They stated that in the event of the loss of cabin pressure, you were responsible for putting an oxygen mask over yourself before assisting other passengers. Now, would you classify this precaution as selfish or indulgent? Absolutely not. It's a safety procedure that can potentially keep you alive.

The same can be said about practicing self-love. Setting standards for how others treat you and putting your needs first are habits that protect your well-being and keep you healthy. When your needs are taken care of, you're able to invest more time and energy in taking care of others. Self-love makes it possible for you to build healthy relationships because you can sincerely love and accept who you are, which means that you won't demand love and acceptance from others.

Speaking about self-compassion, Professor Kristin Neff writes, "Self-compassion involves treating yourself with the same kindness, concern, and support you'd show to a good friend. When faced with difficult life struggles or confronting personal mistakes, failures, and inadequacies, self-compassion responds with kindness rather than harsh self-judgment, recognizing that imperfection is part of the shared human experience" (Neff & Dahm, 2015).

It's not wrong to give yourself the same love and respect you give to others. Yes, this might cause others to feel uncomfortable around you, however, realize that the discomfort they feel has more to do with their own emotional wounds. Misery loves company, and when you no longer think low of yourself, there will be friends and family you can't seem to get along with anymore. You'll need to choose between continuing on your healing journey (even if it means ending unhealthy relationships) or giving in to the social pressure.

If you're interested in deepening the love you have for yourself, be prepared to work for it! It won't be an easy journey, but in the end it will be worth it. One of the techniques that can help you cultivate self-love is mirror work. The following section will explain the technique in more detail.

Step-by-Step Process to Practice Mirror Work

Mirror work is a technique that literally gets you face-to-face with your own image. It's a simple yet incredibly powerful way of coming to terms with who you are and loving the person you see staring back at you in the mirror.

The technique was created by motivational teacher Louise Hay. She found that looking at yourself in the mirror can help you get in touch with your inner self. The purpose of mirror work is to build a stronger relationship with yourself and, over time, cultivate self-love and a healthy self-esteem.

Even though all you need is a mirror, this technique can feel overwhelming. The reflection you see in the mirror can bring up many memories, strong emotions, or negative thoughts you have about yourself. You may feel embarrassed about how you look, unsettled by the eye contact, or angry at yourself for past mistakes and regrets. In her book, *Mirror Work*, Louise Hay explains why staring at a mirror can be unpleasant. She writes, "The mirror reflects back to you the feelings you have about yourself. It makes you immediately aware of where you are resisting and where you are open and flowing" (Hay, 2016).

In other words, looking at yourself in the mirror forces you to be vulnerable. It gives you no room to hide what you think or how you feel about yourself. Of course, this also creates an opportunity to strengthen the relationship you have with yourself by confronting the 'ugly' truth that you have concealed for so many years.

There isn't a rigid set of rules you need to follow when practicing mirror work. However, there are five steps that can help you get the best out of your practice. The five steps are as follows:

Step 1: Show Commitment

It's possible to stare at yourself in front of a mirror and not get anything out of it. What makes mirror work powerful isn't looking at the mirror, but rather opening yourself up emotionally so that you can connect to your soul. Commit yourself to the experience of soul-searching and embracing every aspect of who you are. No, it won't feel comfortable all the time, however, it will bring up thoughts and emotions you have stored deep in your subconscious mind.

So, how can you show commitment? Dedicate a minimum of two minutes a day looking into a mirror and practicing one of the exercises that will be mentioned in the following steps.

Step 2: Create a List of Personalized Affirmations

One of the exercises you can practice while staring at a

mirror is reciting positive affirmations. Simply put, positive affirmations are statements written in the present tense that affirm positive qualities, strengths, and beliefs about who you are. What makes positive affirmations powerful is that they create positive suggestions in your mind. Over time, these suggestions inform how you think about yourself and others. For example, if you're battling with negative self-talk, positive affirmations can counteract those thoughts and slowly change the quality of your internal dialogue.

While you can find thousands of positive affirmations online, it's recommended to create personalized affirmations that target aspects of yourself that you would like to improve. For example, you can create an affirmation based on how you desire to feel about yourself, such as: "I am at peace with myself." Note that the affirmation is positive and written in the present tense. You may also wish to affirm something that you hope to one day display, such as: "I am confident in expressing my needs."

If affirming certain qualities about yourself feels too difficult, choose milder qualities. The point is not to fake something that you don't feel comfortable with yet. For example, staring at yourself in a mirror and saying "I love you" may be difficult to do at this stage. But you can think of a milder affirmation that feels more believable, such as "I accept you for who you are."

You can also refer to this list of positive affirmations when affirming your strengths, desires, and beliefs:

- I am growing.
- Life is getting better for me.
- I am a survivor.
- I am unstoppable.
- I wake up motivated.
- My life is constantly unfolding.
- I am a walking, breathing, talking miracle.
- I inspire everyone who I encounter.
- I am driven to pursue my dreams.
- I am free from the bondage of fear.
- I am healing every day.

Step 3: Validate Your Emotions

It's common to become emotional during the practice of mirror work. You may not even understand where the emotion is coming from. For example, after reciting an affirmation, it may trigger deep sadness or anger. The affirmation only serves as a channel to give you access to deeper parts of your subconscious. Thus, when you speak certain words, they trigger past memories or traumas that haven't yet been healed.

Don't be afraid of your emotions. They are a good indication that the mirror is doing its job! You're supposed to cry, get angry, laugh, or feel embarrassed, because these emotions must be released in order to process pain. When you feel an emotion bubbling up within you, invite it to come forward and spend a few minutes with you. You can speak directly to the emotion and say, "I can feel you, anger. It's okay to come forward." When your emotion reveals itself, allow it to have its moment. Don't hold back how you feel or what comes naturally to you at that moment. Validate the emotion as though you were comforting your younger self. Say to yourself, "I get it. I'm here for you."

Step 4: Ground Yourself in Your Body

Mirror work can get extremely intense, particularly if traumatic wounds have resurfaced. In this place of vulnerability, it's important to show yourself compassion and remain present in your body. Ideally, you want to offer positive reassurance while avoiding being caught up in the memory and drifting to the past. One of the ways to remain present in your body is to ground yourself through gentle touch.

Touch awakens your senses and keeps you connected to the moment. It's also a great way to self-soothe and reduce feelings of being exposed or ashamed. While staring at the mirror, give yourself a warm hug, stroke your arms, place your hand over your heart, touch your face, or any other loving touch that can make you feel safe. While touching yourself, you can even repeat, "You are not alone. You will get through this."

Step 5: Document the Experience

After you have completed your practice, take a few minutes to journal about your experience. Write down what came up, what triggered it, and the emotional experience that followed. If there was something new that you learned about yourself, or any epiphanies you had, write these down too. As time goes on, you'll be able to track your healing process by reading your journal and looking at how far you have come.

While mirror work is centered around the relationship you have with yourself, in the long run it can also improve the relationship you have with others. By gaining more awareness of who you are and learning to love the person you see in the mirror, your connections with others become stronger and more meaningful too!

Chapter Takeaways

- You're prone to repeating relationship patterns you learned growing up in your adult relationships. If you didn't receive the affection you needed, the possibility of opening yourself up to love as an adult can be scary.
- Desiring healthy relationships doesn't necessarily mean you'll attract secure and well-adjusted people, especially if you're holding on to old defense mechanisms, like shutting down or creating distance between yourself and others.
- Cultivating healthy relationships is a process that begins with you; you need to first get to know yourself and accept your strengths and weaknesses before you can open yourself to others.
- Attracting loving relationships becomes easier when you have first developed self-love and can stand up for yourself. Self-love isn't selfish or indulgent, but rather a necessary habit to protect your overall well-being. It's only after you have poured into your own cup that you can pour into others'.

6

Discovering Your Core Values and Raising Your Standards

"It is not until you change your identity to match your life blueprint that you will understand why everything in the past never worked."

— SHANNON L. ALDER

This chapter talks about:

- How your beliefs shape your life experiences
- How to identify your core values
- How raising your standards helps you become the best version of yourself

What Do You Believe In?

Whenever you meet a stranger, you get an opportunity to express who you are. Typically, without even knowing it, your attitudes and behaviors do most of the speaking on your behalf.

Research has shown that people make their first impression of you based on nonverbal communication, like how you carry yourself and the energy you bring into a room.

You don't have to be a human behavioral scientist to spot an insecure person in a crowded room. They're the person who arrives late to make an entrance, struggles to make eye contact or engage in meaningful conversation, and shows signs of high agreeableness, like showing support for what everyone says but failing to offer their own insight. On the other side of the spectrum, they might reveal their insecurity by displaying domineering behavior (standing over people), cutting others off when speaking, and showing disinterest when they're not the center of attention.

The traits and behaviors you display to others say a lot about how you feel about yourself. When you think low of yourself, you tend to act in ways that reinforce your inferiority complex. Skills like setting healthy boundaries or communicating assertively may not have the intended effects on your relationships because on a deeper soul level, you're dealing with a sense of low self-worth.

This is why techniques like confronting your negative beliefs (turn to Chapter 9) are so important to practice on this healing journey. They allow you to take a good look at who you are and ask tough questions like, "What do I believe in?" What you believe in ends up becoming who you are. Your reality is merely a reflection of the quality of your thoughts about yourself and others. This is because your thoughts inform what you consider to be true about people, the world, and your past, as well as your future.

Consider a belief like, "I'm not worthy of love." The belief might be based on a series of past traumatic relationships that left you feeling betrayed and emotionally wounded. Believing that you're not worthy of love comes with an implication: You will subconsciously look for evidence—or create an environment—that reinforces what you believe is the truth. In other words, every experience you have will be seen and evaluated based on the filter that you are unworthy of love.

Imagine how this belief might affect your relationships with others. Regardless of how much love they show you and how often they express their appreciation or respect your boundaries, your mind will discount or overlook any kind of information that doesn't support your belief. Instead, it will work tirelessly to find evidence of the relationship being wrong or the person not being the right fit for you.

Therefore, if you desire to change the first impression that others have of you, or perhaps improve the quality of your relationships, then the first thing to do is assess the quality of your beliefs. What kind of negative suggestions are you constantly feeding yourself? When you meet people, what kind of interactions are you subconsciously expecting? You may not be able to control what happens to you, but you can control how you perceive situations and how they shape you. The power lies in your beliefs.

Core Values: The Center of Your Belief System

A belief system is a network of beliefs that help you make sense of life, understand how to show up in relationships, and distinguish between acceptable and unacceptable behaviors. Your experience of reality is also predicated on your belief system. In essence, what you like or dislike about yourself, your job, or other people is based on a network of beliefs with which you live by.

Not all beliefs that are part of your belief system stem from childhood. Some of them are a result of good or bad experiences you have had later on in life. Furthermore, not all of your beliefs will be based on moral or religious principles. You may have several that stem from your ideas about gender, sexuality, race, politics, health, education, or how society is structured.

What makes your belief system unique from others is how your beliefs are interconnected with each other (how they form a system). For example, believing that men are dangerous, women are undermined in the workplace, and that true love doesn't exist creates a unique belief system that informs how you interact with the world. Thus, when two strangers meet to form any type of relationship, they each bring along their unique belief systems. At times there are similarities between their systems, and other times there aren't any.

Two strangers who have unresolved childhood trauma may have belief systems that complement each other. As a result, they're able to relate to one another, even when what they're relating to would be considered toxic. For example, someone with an avoidant-dismissive attachment style who believes that love is painful might end up attracting someone with an anxious-preoccupied attachment style who doesn't believe they deserve to be loved. While these two people have slightly different belief systems, they're able to complement each other based on their perceptions about love.

What do belief systems have to do with setting healthy boundaries? The answer is simple. Setting healthy boundaries would be a breeze if you actually believed they were valuable or necessary. The fact that you don't have a lot of healthy boundaries means there are some beliefs that you hold that conflict with the act of setting healthy boundaries. One of those beliefs might be the sense that you need to prove yourself to others. Proving yourself to others means placing their needs above yours, hence the lack of healthy boundaries.

What also makes setting healthy boundaries difficult is the fact that, due to your history, you have never gotten the opportunity to think about or put into effect your core values. Core values are at the heart of your belief system. When you have solid core values, you're able to build a life that aligns with what matters to you most, which includes decisions about work, relationships, and the kinds of goals you pursue.

Core values also influence your sense of right and wrong. When setting boundaries, they dictate where your limits are. And since they're the foundation of your belief system, they predict what you believe about yourself and others. For instance, if you value time, then you'll likely believe in task efficiency, punctuality, and planning. Not knowing what your core values are means that your beliefs aren't anchored to what matters most in your life. Instead, they're subject to shift and change based on your life experiences. This results in constant mood swings, anxiety, and confusion whenever you're faced with difficult circumstances.

The best way to ensure that your healthy boundaries remain stable and consistent over time is to get clear about your core values. Figure out what matters to you most and live your life on that model. When you're clear about your core values, you'll notice that your belief system changes. The new beliefs you adopt will be aligned to the fundamental principles that you hold about life, health, goals, work, and relationships. In the following section, we'll think practically about how to identify core values.

Identify Your Core Values

You made dinner plans with a friend and both of you agreed to meet at 7 p.m. sharp. It's been 45 minutes, and they still haven't shown up. Are you waiting or leaving?

After a month of dating your partner, you find out that they lied about not having kids. Is this a deal breaker, or can it be resolved through a conversation?

Your boss just gave you a performance bonus. Do you put the money toward your retirement or start planning your upcoming vacation?

These questions represent some of the many decisions you

make on a daily basis. Your decisions determine how you interact with the world and reflect what you value most in your work, family, health, and friendships. If you didn't have core values, making decisions would be overwhelming. It would be tough deciding which outcome is best for you because you wouldn't have a blueprint that you live by.

Furthermore, since life will always introduce you to different kinds of people and situations, having core values gives you a greater sense of control. In every relationship or situation, you can make decisions that are consistent with what you believe. This doesn't mean you can control the other person or manipulate a situation to work in your favor, but your values will help you set boundaries so that your interests are taken care of.

The following steps are designed to get you thinking about your core values. Get a pen and paper and go through each step at your own pace.

Step 1: Create a List of Values You Are Already Aware Of

The first step is to create a long list of values that you believe reflect what matters most to you. Try not to think too hard about these values, because later on you'll get the chance to narrow them down. If you can't think of values from the top of your mind, refer to the list below for inspiration:

- productivity
- family
- balance
- hard work

- acceptance
- respect
- beauty
- goal-oriented
- success
- accountability
- security
- growth
- ambition
- purpose
- generosity
- simplicity
- peace
- freedom
- kindness
- commitment
- honesty
- fun
- intelligence
- communication

Step 2: Extract Values From Your Past Experiences

Now that you have a long list of values to work with, go a bit deeper and think of past experiences (extreme highs or lows) that revealed some of your core values. Which values shone through during that joyful or painful time? Think of at least three experiences and add more values to your list.

Step 3: Complete a Self-Assessment

Next, turn to yourself and reflect on your personality, mannerisms, beliefs, and attitudes. Identify a few more values based on the following criteria:

- how you structure your daily routine
- the healthiest relationships in your life
- situations that make you angry
- situations that you complain about
- the ideal life you wish to live
- what it takes for you to feel accomplished

You can also take a trip down memory lane and think about what kind of child or teenager you were, how you spent most of your time, and the kinds of interactions that made you sad or happy. Write down values that are illustrated by some of these childhood memories.

Step 4: Create Groups and Highlight Central Themes

At this stage, you should have a list of over 20 values. Identify values that are related to each other and group them together. For example, success, ambition, and goal-oriented would fall under one group because they're similar. Do this for all of your values until you have a few groups.

For each group, select a theme that represents all of the values within it. For example, trust might be a theme that represents values like communication, honesty, and accountability. When you're done, every group should have a central theme.

Step 5: Create Your List of Core Values

The final step is to arrange your themes in order of priority, the number one spot being reserved for the most important theme. Here are a few questions to help you identify which themes take the highest priority (Don't forget that each theme represents a group of similar values.):

- Which themes are essential to your life?
- Which themes represent your authentic self?
- Which themes support the building of healthy relationships?
- Which themes support your deepest desires?

There's no limit to how long your list of core values should be. However, when your list is too long (i.e. having more than 10 core values), you'll easily forget what matters most to you, or you may struggle to incorporate all of them into your daily life. The sweet spot is having a list of 5–10 core values.

The bonus step is to create positive statements that can help you memorize each value. These are known as value statements. The most effective value statements include the following qualities:

- consist of inspiring words
- trigger positive emotions
- highlight your strengths
- designed to be meaningful, not perfect

Below is an example of how you write a value statement structured around your theme and associated values:

Theme: Love

Associated values: Compassion, acceptance, support

Value statement: Love is when someone shows compassion for my feelings, accepts me for who I am, and shows up when

I need them most.

Now, go ahead and create value statements for your list of core values!

It's Time to Raise the Standard

Something magical happens when you realize what you value in life—you finally raise your standards!

A standard is an acceptable norm or average that sets a benchmark or expectation. If you had dreams of becoming a doctor, you would need to pursue a medicine degree that takes an average of six years to complete. This is the standard recommended by international institutions for qualifying as a doctor. If you had a goal of losing a few pounds of weight, you would need to reduce your calorie intake and increase physical activity. This standard formula is what your body responds favorably to.

Elon Musk, who's now ranked the richest person in the world, didn't accumulate his wealth and success by sheer luck. He created a standard of excellence that helped him design his daily routine and the amount of hours he would dedicate to his work. His day is organized in five-minute segments, and he's known to work at least 100 hours a week.

When he was establishing his company, Tesla, Musk was known to sleep on the production floor or in the conference room just so he could maximize the amount of productive hours (SCB, 2022). Of course, this kind of lifestyle isn't healthy.

However, what's important to learn about Musk's approach to success is that he consistently practiced behaviors that were his personal benchmark and informed how he ran his businesses and structured his life.

A C student in high school achieves a C on their report card because they invest "C" amount of effort. In contrast, an A student achieves an A on their report card because they invest "A" amount of effort. When both students leave high school, they'll have access to different kinds of opportunities. The C student's options will be limited due to their minimal effort in high school, whereas the A student will have a variety of options to choose from.

This analogy can be applied to your life. If you set "C" standards regarding how others treat you, you'll get "C" treatment. But if you raise your standards and expect more from yourself and others, you'll receive better treatment. Low standards cause you to accept whatever others have to offer without creating a benchmark. This means that they can say or do anything to you or around you and there won't be any consequences for it. However, when you raise your standards, you create a new normal in your life and make it clear what you can and can't tolerate.

Raising your standards also means modeling the kind of behaviors you expect from others. People often learn how to treat you by watching how you treat yourself. For example, if you don't display any self-respect or self-control, people won't be afraid to walk all over you. Whether you're at work, amongst friends, or at home, it's important to be aware of how your attitudes and behaviors come across to others. Unfortunately, you're judged based on what others perceive about you, not your good intentions. As the police warning goes: Anything you do or say can and will be held against you!

Three Ways to Raise Your Standards

It only takes 30 seconds of first meeting you for someone to create a story about you, but seven positive interactions for you to make up for a bad first impression. Based on their perception about your standards (i.e. whether you're somebody with high or low standards) they'll adjust their behaviors and engage with you accordingly. Therefore, it's crucial to create a benchmark for yourself and display behaviors that represent who you are and what you stand for.

If you're tired of attracting the wrong kind of attention or treatment from people, perhaps it's time for you to raise your standards. The following three-step process will show you how:

• Figure Out What You Want

If you aren't clear about the way you want to be treated, then you won't be able to model those behaviors to others. Clarifying what you want will also make it easier to recognize boundary violations and other undesirable behaviors. Write down a list of at least 10 behaviors you would like to adopt. These are the behaviors that will create a benchmark for how others treat you. For example, if you want others to respect you, then you must practice self-respect (and believe you deserve to be respected).

- **Bridge the Gap**

Your standards should always reflect who you desire to be (your future self) so that you're inspired to evolve and become that person. If you assess your life right now, you'll find that there's a gap between your present and future self. Your present self is the person you are right now. This version of you also has standards, however, they're not a reflection of who you desire to be—the future self. Write a letter to your future self expressing how you would like others to see you. Describe scenarios at work, amongst your friends, and with family that would make you feel accepted and respected.

You can also bridge the gap, you can ask yourself sobering questions about your current standards and what needs to change in order to become a better person. Here are a few questions to start you off:

- What are three standards that are keeping you stuck in the past?
- What are three standards that reinforce the same unhealthy relationship patterns?
- What standards do you maintain at work? How might these standards be holding you back?
- What standards do you maintain about your health? How might these be compromising your physical well-being?
- What standards did you learn from other people (e.g. parents, coworkers, friends, ex-partners, etc.) that are negatively impacting your life?

The aim with bridging the gap is to assess areas where you can improve your standards. For example, you might find that you have great work and dating standards, but when it comes to your health and family, you need to raise your standards. Furthermore, while completing the self-assessment, you may find standards that are toxic and can no longer be maintained. Be honest about what you're not willing to tolerate anymore and why it's important for you to make these changes.

- **Find the Right Mentors**

Now that you're clear about what you want and understand what it will take to bridge the gap, the next step is to find great mentors. The beauty about standards is that you can always find a person who exemplifies what you desire to become or display. Think about role models like Michelle Obama, Serena Williams, or Warren Buffett. These individuals may be different, but what they have in common is that they're all living based on their highest standards—and it shows in their mindsets, characters, and professional lives.

Find a few people who exemplify the kind of standards you hope to develop. The purpose is not to idolize them, but to draw inspiration from their journeys. If you can't think of any celebrity figure, think about people who you have encountered in your life who left a positive impact on you. What was it about your parents, school teacher, or football coach that you admire and would like to embody?

When you have completed these three steps, it's time to take action by developing daily or weekly rituals. Rituals are simply behaviors carried out the same way, at the same time, which support the new standards you have set for yourself. To make your rituals effective, ensure they're small, easy to follow, and don't require a lot of time and money. For example, waking up at 6:30 a.m. and meditating for 10 minutes is a great way to cultivate inner peace.

Challenge yourself to explore different rituals until you find those that accommodate your lifestyle and help you become a better person.

Chapter Takeaways

- People treat you as well as you treat yourself. Whenever you're engaging with people, be aware of how others might perceive you. Consider how your attitudes and behaviors come across, and make the best first impression!
- Your belief system is a network of beliefs that help you interpret the world. If your beliefs are negative, your behaviors will be negative too. It's only when you start challenging your beliefs that you can change how you act, think, or show up in the world.
- At the heart of your belief system are your core values. These are the ideas or principles that matter most to you. When you make decisions based on your core values, you're able to live a life that's consistent with what you believe.
- Discovering your core values helps you create personal standards or benchmarks in various aspects of your life. These standards teach others how to relate to you and how much respect to show you. However, the most important part about setting personal standards is that you get to

adopt new behaviors that help you become the best version of yourself.

7

Boundaries in Relationships

*"Evaluating the benefits and drawbacks of any relation-
ship is your responsibility. You do not have to passively
accept what is brought to you. You can choose."*

— DEBORAH DAY

This chapter talks about:

- How to maintain your individuality in relationships by
  going through the process of individuation
- How to start a conversation about boundaries with friends,
  romantic partners, and family members

Embrace the Process of Individuation

Tanya and Zach decided to go for couple's therapy after two
years of being together. Both of them felt ready for marriage,
except they kept on getting into the same kinds of struggles
for power.

Zach was an assertive, straight-talking man in his mid 30s who was raised in a liberal household, where mutual respect lay the foundation for his relationships with his parents. He grew up with a love for accounting and with the support of his parents, he climbed the corporate ladder and became one of the youngest directors at his company.

What made him fall in love with Tanya was her kind and agreeable nature—but these traits also became what sparked many arguments. "Whenever I ask her to make a decision," Zach told the therapist, "she always goes with what I like instead of making her own choices."

Tanya was a typical people-pleaser who felt uncomfortable speaking up for herself. She was raised by strict parents who restricted many of her freedoms and kept a close watch on everything she did. From an early age, she learned that being agreeable was the best way to relate to her parents and get along with others. When she met Zach, this relationship pattern played out once again, but unfortunately it created more tension than harmony in their relationship.

Observing their relationship, the therapist realized that most of their conflict was due to their patterns of individuation. Psychoanalyst Carl Jung discovered the concept of individuation, which is the process of forming a separate identity from others and realizing who you are. This is an ongoing process that begins from infancy and continues into adulthood, and is most noticeable in how people relate with one another.

One of the signs of individuation is developing a separate

identity from your friends and family. In other words, you seek to find out what your strengths and weaknesses are, what kind of personality you have, and what you desire out of life. During this process of exploration, you may discover hidden aspects of your identity that weren't revealed as a child. As you can imagine, going on this journey takes a lot of courage because what you might learn about yourself could change the nature of your relationships.

Parents are typically responsible for helping their children along the process of individuation in order to prepare them for life as an independent adult. However, not all parents take their children through this journey, hence the dynamic between Tanya and Zach. Tanya's strict parents imposed their own beliefs and expectations on their daughter, which made self-realization impossible. Even in her adult life, Tanya struggled to develop an independent identity from her romantic partners because she was never encouraged to.

On the other hand, Zach's parents raised him to have a healthy sense of autonomy from a young age. They created an environment where he felt safe to voice his opinions and make important decisions for his life, such as deciding to pursue a career in finance. Knowing that he was supported by his parents gave Zach the self-confidence to discover who he was and build a stable life for himself.

Since relationships are a necessary part of growing up and living a fulfilling life, it's important to undergo the process of individuation to form a separate identity from others. Perhaps you grew up in a family similar to Tanya's, where you weren't encouraged to find your voice, communicate your needs, and express your individuality. Not having the support of your parents in discovering who you are meant that you depended on others for validation: At work this might show up as a lack of assertiveness, and in romantic relationships it might show up as passivity or neediness.

The good news is that it's never too late to continue the process of individuation and create an independent identity from your parents or people who you have deep emotional ties with.

Three Stages of Individuation

If you desire to become your own person and gain the confidence to think, feel, and behave in ways that are authentic to you, then it's important to go through the process of individuation. Depending on how restrictive your past relationships were, there may still be aspects of your identity that are tied to your parents' or ex-lovers' thoughts, beliefs, and values. You can redeem these aspects of your identity by following the three stages of individuation: declaring, separating, and reconnecting.

Declaring

The first stage is to declare your freedom from whomever your identity has been tied to for all these years. You can make this declaration to yourself by stating that you're severing the emotional ties that have kept you enmeshed with another person's ideas, thoughts, and feelings.

This stage can involve mirror work, where you look at yourself in the mirror and declare your freedom out loud. You can also write letters to yourself in a journal and explain the decision you're making and why you have chosen to cut emotional ties. It isn't necessary to share your declaration with the person you're emotionally separating from, although if you do, ensure that you don't overly explain yourself or get caught up in blackmail and other forms of manipulation.

Declaring your freedom might sound like this:

> *"I'm going through a process of making positive changes in my life and relationships. I take responsibility for not always standing up for myself, expressing my emotions, and protecting my boundaries. I have decided that in order to continue my personal evolution and maintain the health of this relationship, I have to become more independent and stand on my own. This doesn't mean I don't love you, however, I need to fight for myself and my own wishes more than I depend on others to carry me."*

Separating

The second stage of individuation is the actual separation. You can interpret this separation in two ways. First, it could be setting healthy boundaries with the other person so that you have the space to grow and explore who you are. Alternatively, if the relationship no longer feels safe, you can make a physical separation and request some time apart. Whether you decide to set healthy boundaries or create physical distance, it's important to disconnect emotionally—until you have created a life for yourself.

The purpose of separating isn't to hurt the person who you have been enmeshed with, but instead to get clear on who you are and take full responsibility for your life. It's also during this stage of separation that you're able to reflect on your relationship dynamic and identify harmful patterns of behavior like codependency, seeking validation, or using the other person to distract you from your feelings of loneliness.

In an article titled *How to Individuate*, author Jake Eagle recounts a story about a grown child who was finally ready to separate from their parents. Below is their story of how the process of separation occurred (Eagle, 2011):

> *"I haven't lived with my parents for years, but I called them every week. I always asked about them, but they never asked about me. Or, if they did, it was because they wanted to tell me what I should be doing in some area of my life. I got sick of it, so I told my parents that if they wanted to know how I was they should call me. I told them I was going to stop calling them for a while. And I did. And they never called me. This caused me to rethink my relationship with them. I struggled to accept that my parents didn't reach out to me, but only after experiencing this did I begin to understand myself much better. Someday I will reach out to my parents, but not until their response is less important to me."*

Reconnecting

The last stage of individuation is reconnecting to those whom you separated from. Please note that in some cases, especially when the relationship was toxic or no longer felt safe, reconnecting may not be possible. However, you won't know for sure until you have gone through the first and second stage.

If the relationship is salvageable, it means that there's commitment from both parties to respect each other's autonomy. In other words, the person who felt subjected to must commit to respecting your boundaries and giving you the space to think for yourself and lead a separate life. Think of this as a new chapter in your relationship, where both of you get to relearn each other and operate under a new vision (refer to Chapter 4).

If coming to a mutual agreement is difficult (i.e. the other person refuses to cooperate or respect your new boundaries), then it may be necessary to take your relationship back to the separation stage. Reuniting with someone who isn't willing to change will recreate the same patterns of dependency that you don't desire anymore. There will also be some people whom you reconnect with but continue to maintain your distance from. These may be family members who you can't walk away from but also can't allow full access into your life.

This three-stage individuation process is generally directed toward your parents, because the parent-child relationship is the primary one that sets the tone for all other relationships in your life. If your parents are deceased, or maybe you're afraid of making the separation, then you'll most likely project the unresolved issues from your parent-child relationship onto your romantic relationships. For example, if your parents were emotionally unavailable, you may be emotionally needy in your romantic relationships.

The reason why it's so important to separate from your parents is to accept that how they raised you was the best they could do with what they knew at the time. Their parenting was in no way a reflection on who you are. The lack of unconditional love from your parents didn't make you unlovable or unworthy of receiving love. Therefore, since your parents' actions and behaviors had very little to do with you as a person, you don't need to reinforce those patterns in your adult relationships.

Communicating Boundaries With Friends

Friendships tend to change over time as the people who are part of the friendship evolve. The kind of friendship expectations you had when you were in high school are different from what you expect in your friendships at this stage of your life. Plus, from each friendship dynamic, you may desire something different. For example, there might be a friend you call whenever you want to socialize, and another friend you call whenever you want to have deep meaningful conversations. Both friendships are valuable in their own way because they respond to your friendship needs.

While each friendship may look different, there are standards that healthy friendships must uphold. These standards are:

- **Being emotionally available for each other.** Even though there are many things that fight for your attention, it's important to pay attention to how your friends are coping and what their needs are, and vice versa. Having concern for one another's well-being is what builds mutual connection.
- **Having a balance of give-and-take.** Reciprocity is essential to healthy friendships because it ensures that both people's needs are considered and taken care of. One-sided friendships often consist of one person who always gives and another who always takes. There can be no harmony in these types of friendships due to one person who has overextended themselves.
- **Offering support during difficult times.** Life isn't always full of joyful moments, and as much as you can celebrate with your friends, you also want to count on them to hold your hand during tough times. Support might look different for each of your friendships. For example, you might approach some people for emotional support and others to teach you skills or share their knowledge. What matters is knowing that you can rely on your friends to carry you during moments of weakness, and vice versa.
- **Feeling safe to be vulnerable.** Healthy friendships offer a psychologically safe space where you can share your thoughts and emotions without feeling judged or exposed. Sharing personal information must be a mutual agreement and something that you both do freely in order to build a strong connection. The inability to be vulnerable could be an indicator of a lack of trust.
- **Maintaining a level of consistency.** Friendships are not static; they ebb and flow as time passes by. However,

healthy friendships are built on values, traditions, and common practices that make them feel stable and reliable. For example, friends might agree to meet up at least once a month for a catchup or check up on each other over text once a week. These small practices are what keep friendships intact.

There will be moments when you're forced to set boundaries with friends. This isn't always a sign that your friendship is in trouble or that your friend is toxic. As we have mentioned in earlier chapters, even good-intentioned people sometimes violate our boundaries. There are many reasons why setting boundaries would be necessary. Some of those include:

- You're overwhelmed with personal responsibilities and don't have the bandwidth to be there for your friend.
- You have gone through a life transition and your priorities have changed. You're no longer available to hang out like you used to or engage in the types of activities you and a friend used to enjoy.
- The friendship is one-sided and you often find yourself investing more time and energy into maintaining the friendship than your friend.
- You don't feel comfortable sharing personal information with your friend. This could be due to a number of reasons. For instance, the friendship may be new, trust could have been broken in the past, or perhaps your friend is secretive and doesn't share much about themselves.
- You struggle to keep up with your friend's expectations. As much as you desire to respond to their needs, you tend to feel overwhelmed by how much they expect from you.

For example, having a friend who wants to hang out every weekend or expects you to help them make decisions about their own life.

Some boundary violations may be obvious, and others will require you to trust your gut instinct. You can also think about how the behavior committed made you feel. That could be a good indication of a boundary violation. When communicating your boundaries with friends, remember these important tips:

- **Be clear and straightforward.** Get to the point and explain what happened and how it made you feel. If possible, avoid making assumptions or accusations. Simply state the boundary that was crossed and a way forward that both of you can take.
- **Create an atmosphere for open dialogue.** After communicating your issue, give your friend an opportunity to speak and share what's on their mind. They may want to clarify any misunderstandings that have occurred. Seek to understand where they may have been coming from or how they may have been feeling at the time. Being able to talk freely about your experiences can strengthen your friendship.
- **Emphasize how much you value the friendship.** Communicating your boundaries doesn't need to be a combative situation. After all, the aim isn't to damage your friendship, but to make it stronger. Before and after you define the consequences, express how committed you are to making the friendship work and how much you care about your friend.

Setting boundaries in friendships is all about communicating how your needs have changed and how you would like your friends to treat you moving forward. The aim is never to end a friendship, but to make your needs clearer. In romantic relationships, the type of boundaries you set looks a bit different, especially earlier on during the dating stage!

How to Talk About Boundaries During the Dating Stage

How would you respond if the man or woman you had only known for a week asked you to send nudes? Or what would you say if the man or woman you had recently started dating asked to borrow a large sum of money?

Setting boundaries in the early stages of dating can feel awkward because you're forced to communicate your limits with somebody you barely know. If you have a tendency to people-please, you might fear that setting boundaries so early may cause them to run away or have a negative perception about you.

The truth is that boundaries are a lifesaver when it comes to screening singles in the dating scene. They protect your interests and ensure that the people you eventually allow into your life understand how to treat you. Healthy boundaries aren't a mood killer. In fact, they can strengthen the attraction between you and your partner since both of your needs are being met. Plus, if you have experienced abusive relationships in the past, having boundaries in place protects you from re-traumatization.

Communicating boundaries with a romantic partner sounds and looks similar to how you would communicate boundaries with anyone else. Nevertheless, there are a few guidelines that will make approaching this situation less daunting:

- **Speak about your boundaries as soon as possible.** Ideally, you want to set the ground rules for your romantic relationship after the first few dates, when you begin to take the other person seriously. This doesn't have to be a formal conversation; it can be a topic that you bring up on a fun date. For instance, you might start the conversation by asking, "What's important for you in a relationship?"
- **Use "I" statements.** The purpose of dating is to get to know someone better. Therefore, it's normal to share your likes and dislikes. If your partner has violated one of your boundaries, there's a good chance that they weren't even aware of it. Use "I" statements to teach your partner what you like and dislike. You might say, "When you make last-minute plans, I don't feel considered."
- **Share your sexual boundaries before you engage in sex.** Good sex is all about consent. When there's no consent, the act becomes a sexual violation. Be clear ahead of time about your sexual boundaries. You may even want to have an open discussion about your sexual beliefs, like waiting until a relationship reaches a certain milestone before having sex or practicing safe sex by wearing condoms. Remember that both you and your partner can withdraw consent at any time, so check in with each other regularly to see if your sexual boundaries are being upheld.
- **Be clear about your non-negotiables.** It's normal to

enter a new romantic relationship with non-negotiables, especially if you're living based on your core values. Your partner should know what you need in order to feel safe and honored in the relationship. In some cases your partner may not be willing to accept your non-negotiables, and this could make them walk away. Don't see this as a bad sign. It simply means that you weren't compatible in the first place.

- **Look out for yourself.** It's common for new lovers to become so besotted with each other that they forget to protect their own interests. For a relationship to make it past the honeymoon phase, both you and your partner must feel comfortable being yourselves and continuing to live separate lives, together. Neither of you should feel like you're compromising yourselves by staying in the relationship.

Your mindset during the dating process is another factor to consider. Be careful about the beliefs you hold about yourself, such as thinking you're not good enough to be treated a certain way. Your mindset will also affect your behaviors. If you think low of yourself, it will be evident in how you carry yourself on each date, as well as how loose your boundaries are. Remember, you teach people how to treat you through your behaviors. Act like a king or queen, and you will be treated like one!

Unlike bad dates, you can't walk away as easily from family. Nevertheless, your difficult family members must be held accountable for boundary violations just like any other relationship in your life.

Setting Clear Boundaries With Difficult Family Members

What makes setting boundaries with family so hard is the fact that these relationships hold so much value. For instance, as frustrated as you might be with your parent's selfish behavior or manipulative tactics, they will always be your parent. Many people end up excusing bad behavior from family members as a way of ignoring the boundary violation. However, doing this only leads to further hurt in the future.

Abuse or mistreatment of any kind is unacceptable, regardless of who the transgressor may be. It's important to get to the point where your mental, physical, and emotional well-being matter more than what others think or react toward you. Individuation is the first step to figuring out who you are and how you desire to be treated. When you think like an independent person with independent needs, you'll find it a lot easier to protect yourself against unfair or abusive behavior.

Once again, communicating your behaviors with difficult family members will follow the same process as other relationships. However, below are some guidelines that will help you set limits with family members without damaging your relationships:

- **Decide what's best for you.** Take a moment and think about what would make the relationship with a family member feel safe and fulfilling for you. Try not to think about them and their experience, but focus on your unmet needs. Write down a list of these needs, and for each

126

one, set a boundary to protect it. Schedule a time to communicate these boundaries with your family member.

- **Prepare for pushback.** Depending on how long this particular family member has overlooked your needs, they may resist adhering to your boundaries. Don't be tempted to compromise or revert back to how your relationship used to be. Remain calm and level-headed, and repeat the same boundaries. If they violate your boundaries (perhaps to test how serious you are), enforce the appropriate consequence and explain once again why the boundary means so much to you.

- **Know what triggers you, and make the necessary preparations.** Triggers are words, behaviors, or attitudes that cause a negative emotional response. You may already know what triggers you about a family member's actions, however, to protect your state of mind you need to learn how to anticipate these triggers and the best ways to respond. For example, if you suspect that visiting your parents will be stressful, plan ahead of time how long you'll stay there, what topics you'll discuss (and those off the table), and an exit plan if the environment becomes toxic.

- **Practice saying no without explaining yourself.** It isn't always necessary to justify your decisions. It's okay to refuse to do something and not have to feel guilty about it either. Your 'no' doesn't have to be aggressive to be clear. It just needs to sound certain and not as if there's a question mark at the end. Look into a mirror and practice the different ways of saying no. Hear yourself saying no with confidence and assertiveness. Notice what facial expressions or gestures work well when saying no. Play around with this until you feel comfortable saying no without explaining yourself.

- **Create a list of self-care rituals.** For some people, walking away from family isn't an option. This is usually the case when you're taking care of family members. While healthy boundaries will make the relationship feel a lot more stable, you'll need to practice self-care rituals as a way of disconnecting from others and prioritizing your needs. These may include going to the gym, picking up a hobby, journaling, or finding a support group.

Family relationships are complicated, but that doesn't mean that difficult family members aren't held accountable. Everyone who desires to be a part of your life, whether it be a friend or a family member, must be willing to treat you the way that you want to be treated.

Chapter Takeaways

- When you become an adult, you must complete the process of creating a separate identity from your parents. This prevents you from internalizing your parents' beliefs, behaviors, and traumas, and repeating them in new relationships.
- There are three stages of individuation: declaring, separating, and reconnecting. Declaring your freedom is a conscious choice to think of yourself as someone unique rather than a shadow of your parents. Separating is the painful but necessary stage of creating emotional or physical distance in order to begin the journey of self-discovery. Reconnecting occurs after you have built a solid sense of self and are willing to renegotiate the terms of the

relationships.

- Communicating boundaries with friends, romantic partners, or family members is never an easy conversation. However, the sooner you get it done, the more stable and consistent these relationship will be. Always start the conversation with the intention to strengthen your bond, not tear it down. Listen as much as you speak, and be willing to stand up for yourself if necessary.

8

Boundaries at Work

"A boundary shows me where I end and someone else begins, leading me to a sense of ownership. Knowing what I am to own and take responsibility for gives me freedom."

— HENRY CLOUD

This chapter talks about:

- The importance of establishing healthy boundaries with coworkers
- Whether forming friendships at work is a good or bad thing
- How to communicate assertively in a workplace environment

Why Are Boundaries Necessary at Work?

Work relationships are unique in the sense that they aren't based on attraction or compatibility, but rather collaborating on shared goals. Boundaries with coworkers are useful to ensure that you're not taken for granted (doing more work than you ought to), as well as to work in harmony with others.

Many people fail to set boundaries at work because they assume that coworkers know how to behave respectfully and professionally. This assumption leads to poor communication, being overworked, and resentment amongst colleagues. Just like we can't assume our close friends know what we need, we also can't assume that the people we work with know how to treat us.

The benefits of setting boundaries at work are:

- **You earn the respect of your coworkers.** Having boundaries makes you feel a lot more comfortable sharing your thoughts and suggestions with others without the fear of being shut down or judged. Your boundaries can also teach others how to communicate with you respectfully, so that every interaction is constructive.
- **You set the standards of behavior.** People often test how far they can go with behaviors to see what you will and won't tolerate. By setting boundaries, you communicate clear expectations of what you will and won't tolerate, which ends up becoming how others approach and build relationships with you.
- **You get better at resolving conflict.** Unfortunately,

conflict at work can't be ignored like conflict in a friend-ship or romantic relationship. It needs to be addressed immediately so that it doesn't hamper your workflow. Responding to boundary violations with decisive action reduces the back-and-forth and helps you reach a mutual understanding.

- **You can manage your coworkers' expectations.** There's no doubt that you're exceptional at your job, however, you have limits. For instance, working fast doesn't mean you can take on more workload. Your boundaries draw the line with coworkers and protect you from overcommitting yourself.

As beneficial as having boundaries at work is, there's still the fear of what coworkers might think. Tough conversations with people you aren't close to feel awkward, however, just imagine reporting to a manager or working on a team with a coworker who makes you feel small and undervalued. How would this affect your satisfaction at work?

To make the process of setting boundaries at work less over-whelming, the following section will provide you with exam-ples of what your boundaries might look like.

Examples of Work Boundaries

Healthy work relationships start with healthy boundaries. Take a moment and think about how you desire to feel when you walk into the office in the morning or join a Zoom meeting. Now think about how you desire to feel when you're sharing your ideas or making a presentation. These emotions don't just happen. They come after countless attempts at teaching people how to treat you or how to behave around you. If you desire to feel safe, accepted, and valued at work, consider the kinds of boundaries you would need to establish for that to take place.

To get you started on setting work boundaries, there are three areas you can focus on: job responsibilities, interpersonal boundaries, and personal boundaries. Let's look at each area more closely.

Job Responsibility

Your job responsibilities are the duties that come with your specific role. Before you accept the job position, you agree to complete all of your job responsibilities. This is a boundary created by your manager. If you're unclear about what's expected from you, then you can't work to the best of your ability—and this might cause you to violate the boundary that had been set by your manager. To ensure that you're fulfilling your job responsibilities, answer the following questions:

- What tasks do you perform on a daily basis?
- How does your job contribute to the greater good of the company?
- Who do you report to?
- How is your performance measured?
- What are your current work goals?

Once you're settled in the role, you get to set your own boundaries around your job responsibilities. This means creating rules about the way you work and interact with others. Of course, these rules can't go against your company's policies or culture. They should be directed toward improving your work efficiency and achieving your work goals. Here are a few examples of boundaries you can create:

- asking coworkers not to call your phone after hours
- checking and responding to work emails during designated time slots
- declining meeting invitations that have nothing to do with your current work tasks
- saying no to projects until your schedule has cleared up
- approaching your manager when there's an issue you would like to discuss

Interpersonal Boundaries

Interpersonal boundaries are the limits you create with your manager and coworkers. These boundaries are typically centered around communication preferences, like how you would like coworkers to speak to you or resolve conflict. Examples of interpersonal boundaries at work include:

- the tone of voice others use when speaking to you
- the topics you're open to speak about and those off the table
- how to resolve conflict or work amicably when there's tension within the team
- limits about the sharing of personal or company information

Even if your work relationships are going well and you believe there's no need to set interpersonal boundaries, have a discussion with your coworkers about them. This will help you know how to respond if at any point you or your coworkers violate a boundary.

Personal Boundaries

Personal boundaries are those limits you set with yourself to maintain a healthy work-life balance. They protect you from overworking and ensure you invest your time and energy in other aspects of your life too. Examples of personal boundaries include:

- switching off your work phone when you're at home
- leaving your laptop in the office or in the car after work hours
- scheduling five-minute rest breaks throughout your work day
- taking days off and making sure you don't touch any work during that time
- decluttering your email mailbox after every quarter
- updating your resume every six months

Having these boundaries in place won't protect you from boundary violations. However, if you have read Chapter 3, then you have the necessary tools to set effective consequences and hold coworkers accountable. If you feel intimidated or harassed by a coworker, or maybe that your consequences aren't bringing about the desired change, then you should escalate the matter and allow a third party to intervene.

Can Coworkers Be Friends?

A question that many people grapple with is whether or not to be friends with their coworkers. For instance, what happens when you're placed in a team with someone whom you get along with, and even share many interests with? Is your relationship supposed to be kept strictly professional?

It's possible to meet someone at work and find yourselves instantly bonding. Perhaps you know each other, have mutual friends, or are drawn to each other's personalities. Feeling drawn to your coworkers isn't a bad thing. In fact, if you manage work relationships well, you can balance having both platonic and professional relationships at work. The secret, though, is to take things slow—slower than you would a first date!

The reason for taking things slow is simple: Neither of you are at work to make friends. You're there to accomplish shared goals and objectives. It's in your and their best interest to keep the working relationship at a superficial level until you have built respect for each other and understand one another's work standards and behaviors. After having plenty of professional interactions and going through different work situations together, you can assess if you'd like to get to know your coworker on a friendship level.

Below are more guidelines that will help you navigate the process of cultivating friendships at work:

- **Avoid misreading another person's intentions.** It's

polite to smile and be cordial with others at work. Some company cultures may even encourage team bonding events and other social activities. This isn't an indication that you have something in common with your coworker beyond your work duties. Not everyone is open to making friends at work, specifically in competitive environments. Thus, don't be quick to assume that kindness is a sign of friendship.

- **Have as many face-to-face interactions at the beginning.** If you like somebody and would like to get to know them better, take the opportunity to speak to them at work. Avoid sharing personal information about yourself, including your private social media accounts, until you're certain that you trust the other person.

- **Know what (and what not) to talk about.** In some workplaces, employees get to spend a lot of time together. It could be during brainstorming sessions, team projects, or happy hour. It's easy to forget where you are and who you're talking to when you spend many hours with the same people. However, until you're ready to open yourself up to a friendship, maintain your boundaries when it comes to sharing personal information. You'll know that you've overshared when you feel vulnerable or exposed.

- **When it comes to your boss, tread lightly.** The boss-employee relationship is more sensitive than the relationship between coworkers. This is because your boss is your boss. There's a greater level of consideration you need to have in how you present yourself because you want them to respect you and provide a fair evaluation about your work. Plus, you can still have fun and engage with your boss without being their friend.

- **Avoid forming cliques.** Knowing a lot of people at work and cultivating friendships is good. However, remind yourself that you're no longer in high school. You don't need to form cliques or alliances in the office—and you certainly shouldn't be using these friendships as an opportunity to gossip about or alienate other employees. If you find yourself in a routine of hanging out with the same employees at the same spot, break the routine and get to know other members of your team. You also shouldn't feel pressured to act a certain way just so you can relate to a group of employees. Be yourself and maintain your work standards.

Your coworkers can become some of your closest friends. With the right boundaries in place, you can even balance being personal and professional with one another. Nonetheless, you should be careful of work friendships that are one-sided or only feel like a friendship when certain conditions are met. A good rule of thumb is: If it feels forced, the feeling might not be mutual. If you're ever doubtful about where your relationship stands with a coworker, it's also not a bad idea to be upfront and ask them what their intentions are.

Assertiveness at Work

In Chapter 4, we discussed how to communicate boundaries assertively. From a work context, assertiveness goes much deeper than how you articulate yourself. The main benefit of being assertive at work is gaining the respect of your coworkers. Nevertheless, it's still not an easy skill to learn. If you observe many of your work relationships, you'll find very few people who can communicate assertively. Many of them might fall under the passive, passive-aggressive, or aggressive categories. Below are the common characteristics of these types of employees:

- **Passive coworker:** Internalizes their negative emotions to avoid confrontations or making other employees feel bad or guilty. Their conflict resolution strategy is to go with the flow, even when their needs are compromised. They might say, "I don't mind. Let's go with your idea."
- **Passive-aggressive coworker:** Internalizes their negative emotions, but finds subtle ways of releasing their built-up resentment without their true intentions being known. For example, they're notorious for committing acts of sabotage like missing deadlines or failing to show up to a meeting, and making up an excuse for why they "forgot" to follow through.
- **Aggressive coworker:** They'll express their negative emotions without thinking about the impact of their behavior on work relationships, or whether they're managing the situation in a professional way. When resolving conflict, the aggressive coworker tends to speak more than they listen, and they're likely to defend their position even when they discover they're in the wrong.

Assertive employees aren't necessarily born with the confidence to share their opinions and balance their needs and desires with those of others. In fact, it's possible that due to many boundary violations, the passive or passive-aggressive employee taught themselves how to speak up for themselves and be transparent in how they address issues. As much as all the other types of communicators want to be respected at work, it's only the assertive employee who earns true respect due to their direct and human approach to building relationships.

The assertive employee knows that if they want respect from others, they need to show respect too. Now, this is usually straightforward when there's no conflict amongst employees. When conflict ensues, mutual respect goes out of the window, and the assertive employee must find other ways to appeal to their disgruntled coworker and reach some kind of middle ground. The level of maturity that it takes to be calm and level-headed, even when you're not shown the same decency, is part of what makes an assertive employee respectable. They have a way of seeing the bigger picture, which is typically a win-win situation that dissolves the conflict.

If you would like to strengthen your assertive communication skills, there are a few habits that you can start practicing at work:

1. Express Your Opinions Boldly

Assertiveness is deepened when you find ways to validate yourself rather than seeking validation from others. You have to believe within yourself that you're qualified to perform your job and that you have a lot of value to offer your company. These beliefs must be something you know to be true, otherwise, expressing your opinions boldly will make you feel too self-conscious. Each type of communicator will express their opinions differently, but to be more assertive, focus on being direct while maintaining respect in your delivery.

2. Maintain Eye Contact

Eye contact is a nonverbal cue that displays assertiveness. It portrays confidence and helps you hold other people's attention. In many cultures, maintaining eye contact is also a form of respect, particularly to people who have a higher social ranking. If you work in a traditional environment, this may be a great way to show coworkers respect without using words. When looking into someone's eyes, be careful not to stare without blinking (this could be interpreted as a sign of aggressiveness).

3. Be the First to Admit When You Were Wrong

Part of strengthening your work relationships and earning others' trust is being able to admit when you were in the wrong. Don't allow your position at work to make it hard for you to apologize and make amends. Just as you're confident to stand up for what's right, it's important to show your coworkers that you can own up to your mistakes. If the entire team made a mistake, own your part instead of passing the blame.

4. Be Inclusive of Others

It's also important to make sure that those you work with feel seen and accepted. For example, when making decisions, make sure that everyone has added their input. Being accepting of others is a great way to model how you would like coworkers to treat you. Ideally, you also want to be seen and accepted in all matters relating to your work. When coworkers feel seen and accepted by you, they're more likely to behave according to your standards and show you the respect you deserve.

5. Be Quick to Forgive

Another great way to model a standard is when it comes to forgiveness. Tension often remains in a team or department long after the conflict has been resolved. This can negatively affect teamwork and the general mood in the atmosphere. If you want to work in a harmonious environment, create a standard by being quick to forgive others. Once the disagreement has been settled, be deliberate in keeping the lines of communication open. Make sure that no one feels alienated or ganged up on, and that the team is able to recover and get back to a healthy space.

You'll find that it's easier to be assertive with other assertive communicators at work. However, when you're dealing with a passive or aggressive communicator, you can lose control of your emotions. What often helps when interacting with non-assertive communicators is to prepare yourself for these encounters. At home, spend time rehearsing what passive and aggressive language sounds like so that you can pick up on a coworker's style of communication.

After you have identified a non-assertive communicator, take a moment to tune into your own emotions. Figure out how you're feeling and what you need at that moment. If you don't feel confident enough to engage in the conversation, you can set an immediate boundary. You might say, "I hear what you're saying, but I don't think I'm getting through to you. Can we reschedule this conversation for another time?" If you agree to engage, remember that a conversation includes back-and-forth. Be willing to listen and validate their experiences, and request the same decency in return.

It's also important to remember that some people might never understand where you're coming from despite your attempts to explain your position. It's okay to not win over every coworker or reach a point where you can squash conflict. You're only responsible for your actions and reactions, not how others act or react towards you. Having said all of this, below are a few tips on how to communicate with the passive, passive-aggressive, and aggressive coworker:

If you want to get through to an aggressive coworker, remember the following:

- **Acknowledge their feelings, even when they don't acknowledge yours.** Aggressive coworkers enter a conversation already having high walls. They're so sensitive to criticism or rejection that anything can send them into attack mode. Make them feel more calm by acknowledging how they feel and emphasizing that you're willing to listen and hopefully reach a win-win situation by the end of the conversation.
- **Take a moment to pause before responding to an emotional outburst.** It's important to calm yourself down and make sure you're feeling strong before responding to an outburst. Responding immediately might cause you to escalate your voice or say something you don't mean. If

you start to feel like you're acting out of character, it's okay to draw a boundary immediately and walk away.

- **Be intentional about finding common ground.** You don't have to give an aggressive coworker what they're looking for, which is a fight. Go into the conversation being clear about your intentions of understanding where they're coming from and walking away having reached a settlement. It might also be necessary to repeat several times during the conversation that you desire to understand where they're coming from and come to a reasonable solution.

Speaking to passive and passive-aggressive coworkers requires a different strategy. Here are a few pointers that will help you get through to them:

- **Encourage them to share their opinions.** Both passive and passive-aggressive coworkers are afraid of being upfront about what they're thinking or feeling. You may need to encourage them to speak freely, especially if you notice that you've been speaking for a long time. You can also read their body language and point out that they're looking confused, uncomfortable, or like they want to say something.
- **Use nonverbal communication to show openness.** It takes a lot of reassurance for passive coworkers to warm up to others. When you're speaking, be mindful of your nonverbal cues, like your facial expressions or gestures. Communicate positive body language by nodding, smiling, making eye contact, and reacting when they make a joke or say something interesting.

- **Show that you accept them for who they are.** Passive and passive-aggressive coworkers are aware of how their lack of assertiveness makes them appear to others. They're also more alert to boundary violations because of their lack of self-defense skills. When communicating, show them respect by giving them an opportunity to speak and having the conversation at their own pace. Never push or insist on them doing something that makes them uncomfortable, like asking for their opinion in front of a group of people.

As you can tell, not everybody at work communicates in the same way. However, the advantage of being an assertive communicator is that you can place yourself in other coworkers' shoes and communicate in a style that makes them feel comfortable.

Chapter Takeaways

- Work relationships are unique because what brings you together isn't a mutual connection, but rather shared goals and objectives. Therefore, what matters most in these types of relationships isn't being emotionally validated, but being respected.
- It's important to create work standards around your job responsibilities, interpersonal boundaries, and personal boundaries. These will create expectations regarding how you work or structure your work day, the acceptable and unacceptable forms of communication with coworkers, and healthy limits to create a good work-life balance.
- Even though forming friendships at work isn't wrong, be careful about how much you share about yourself during

the early stages of getting to know coworkers. Ideally, you want to establish a professional relationship with other employees and iron out any boundary issues or expectations before you can invite each other into your personal lives.

- Assertiveness at work can help you earn the respect of your peers and model the kinds of behaviors you would like others to show you. Being assertive entering conversations with your guard down, being open to listen and admit mistakes, and being intentional about finding common ground.

9

Boundaries Around Social Media

"Don't say anything online that you wouldn't want plastered on a billboard with your face on it."

— ERIN BURY

This chapter talks about:

- Why online privacy should be a priority when sharing data online
- The benefits of creating social media boundaries for your mental health
- How oversharing can cost you your job, and how to avoid it at all costs

The Importance of Online Privacy

In Chapter 1, we discussed how you can set boundaries around your privacy. In this chapter, we'll explore the different ways that you can protect your privacy online. It can be difficult to explain online privacy, because technically no one else has access to your tech gadgets besides you. However, even when you have secure passwords and restricted access to your accounts, your digital footprint can still be traced. This means that people are always keeping tabs on you and your content, as well as your data.

Just because you share information online doesn't mean it should be accessible to everyone. Personal data is the term used to describe information that identifies an individual, which might include (but is not limited to) your cell phone number, home address, company address, banking information, etc. You have the right to keep this type of data private, or in some instances choose who you would like to share it with.

If you're somebody who naturally enjoys their privacy at home, then your online activity doesn't need to be any different. Psychological safety still applies in digital spaces, as it does in your relationships. For example, while networking on social media, you deserve to feel free to share your opinions without being trolled or bullied. Although, even when you do experience harassment of any kind, you have the right to enforce consequences. Of course, the boundaries and consequences you establish online will look different to those you establish in your relationships. However, the sense of safety and contentment you feel will be the same.

Take a moment to create a list of your favorite or go-to mobile apps and websites where you have a registered account. For each app or website, write down the type of personal data you have stored there. It could be your cell phone number, email address, banking details, home address, relationship status, educational history, credit profile, social security number, etc. Looking at your list, you can see just how important maintaining your privacy truly is. The more privacy you have, the easier it is to protect your identity online.

Your homework is to go down the list, log into every app or website, and check your privacy or security settings once again. Perhaps when you registered an account on that platform, you were unaware of the importance of your personal data. Now that you know what these platforms have access to, you can adjust your privacy permissions according to how much you're willing to share. It's also good to be on the lookout for privacy policy updates and to take time to read them so you can ensure there are no privacy violations.

How to Set Up Social Media Boundaries

Social media boundaries aren't necessarily created to keep people out—you can simply use the block button or restrict access to your social media accounts for that. Instead, the boundaries you establish around your social media usage are created to protect your mental health.

You have probably noticed how excessive social media consumption can take a toll on your mental health. However, this doesn't mean that social media is completely bad for you. There's no better way to stay connected with loved ones, build successful businesses, and stay updated on the latest world events than through social media. Nevertheless, if you don't create limits for yourself, then your use of social media becomes toxic. Below are some of the dangers of not having social media boundaries:

- **You can become addicted.** Social media can be addictive because of its effects on your mood. This partly has to do with the instant gratification you receive when you get a 'like' or scroll down an endless feed full of curated content.
- **It limits real life social behavior.** When you're so accustomed to online engagement, it can make real life encounters feel unnatural. Online relationships can also be superficial at times, since you never get to fully discover who the person on the other side of the screen is, or how they're truly feeling.
- **You tend to compare yourself to others.** What's considered a normal life online is often not a realistic goal that you can aim at. For example, in real life it takes more than six months to make millions of dollars, find a soulmate, or buy a dream home. Therefore, when you're wrapped up in the illusions fed by social media, you can start to resent your real life.
- **You become distracted from your daily tasks.** It's easy to lose track of time when you're going through social media. Most platforms are designed to keep you engaged for as long as possible, which makes it difficult to log out once you're online. You can find yourself being easily distracted from your tasks, or performing tasks mindlessly because the real focus is on the content you're watching.
- **You find it difficult to fall asleep at night.** One of the causes of poor sleep is increased screen time before bed. Researchers have found that the blue light emitted from devices keeps your body awake and delays the natural

process of sleep. Taking your devices with you to bed can also keep your mind running and make it harder for it to calm down.

So, what are the boundaries you can establish for yourself to monitor your social media usage and protect your mental health? Consider the following suggestions:

- **Technology-free Sundays:** Are Sundays your rest days? Good! This means that you don't need to be scrolling on your social media either. True rest is about being present and practicing self-care, not checking in on what's happening around the world.
- **Technology curfews:** During the week, you can also limit your social media usage by setting a curfew. For instance, after 8 p.m. you can close your laptop, switch off your TV, and put your phone on silent. Disengaging from technology at least an hour before bed will also improve the quality of your sleep!
- **Put your cell phone away when you're with other people:** Answering text messages, creating content, or responding to notifications can be considered rude when you're having a conversation with someone. Not only that, it can also make it harder to pay attention to what they're saying.
- **Conduct a friendship audit:** Go through the list of people you follow on each social media platform and do a purge! Look specifically for accounts that show harmful content and those that make you feel bad about yourself. Ideally, you don't want to be exposed to any content that doesn't align with your core values or the type of lifestyle

you live.

- **Put yourself on a timer:** Like any other task, add "check social media" on your calendar. Dedicate an amount of time to checking your social media, and once that time lapses, switch to another task.
- **Take time getting to know strangers:** Be mindful of the information you disclose to strangers online. It's never wise to share too much about yourself before meeting face-to-face and having a real life encounter. Get to know who they are offline before investing your time, money, and energy into the relationship.

Be Careful Not to Overshare

Oversharing can be defined as sharing inappropriate or compromising information online. On social media, it would be sharing content that might offend your followers, or that is too personal to share on public platforms (even if your social media accounts are private).

Yes, it's true that social media gives you the freedom to express your views, but what happens when these views re-trigger your trauma, create insecurities, or cost you your job? For example, in past decades, we have read many stories of professionals being fired over racist, homophobic, or violent social media posts. This is because HR departments are now taking social media activity into consideration during the hiring process. Not only can oversharing negatively impact your professional life, it can also lead to an increase in frustration and emotional posting (this is particularly true when you notice that your content is receiving traction).

The cycle often begins with an angry tweet or revealing post that gets a lot of likes or reposts. Perhaps you said something controversial, political, or shared a tragic story about your life. Seeing the positive reaction from the post creates a desire for more validation, until you find yourself desperate for constant attention and reassurance from others—even if it means baring your soul on a public platform.

Giving away so much information about yourself simply to satisfy the demands of others isn't safe, nor is it good for your mental health. You shouldn't feel like you owe others your personal life stories or that in order to be accepted, you need to expose sensitive details about your life. Social media connections can't compensate for real life connections, and sometimes oversharing can be a sign of lack of real support. This doesn't mean that you should delete your social media or limit your engagement. All it means is to be aware that your life shouldn't live on the internet.

Below are some of the tips to avoid oversharing on social media:

- **Decide which platforms are for personal and professional use.** Each social media platform has its own expectations when it comes to creating content. TikTok is great for creating short videos, Instagram is a place to share photos, and LinkedIn is where professionals meet to share knowledge. Ensure that the content you share is appropriate for the platform it's uploaded on.
- **Decide whether content is suitable as a post.** Not every idea or experience you have is shareable. There are some

stories that are too sensitive to be broadcasted on a post, or may be taken out of context. Consider how the post will be received by others, how they might react, and if it offers enough value to share.

- **Avoid posting when you're emotional.** It's never wise to post when you're not in the right frame of mind. This may include when you're angry or under the influence of drugs or alcohol. What you post can be used against you, even if you didn't mean to hurt anyone. As a rule of thumb, write down what you intend on posting on a notepad and wait a few hours before making the decision to post it.

- **Be mindful of the groups and forums you're associated with.** Sometimes it's not what you say that gets you in hot water, but the controversial people, groups, or forums you're associated with. Moreover, if you have your company logo on your profile and post content that's questionable, people can associate what you say with your company's reputation.

- **Do a Google search on yourself.** Type your name into Google and see what search results come up. If there's any information that can be used against you or discredits the person you are today, make sure you delete it. You can also adjust your privacy settings on websites you're subscribed to so that you can manage your online reputation.

In a world where content is in high demand, it can be tempting to become an open book and share intimate details about yourself. If sharing personal information is part of your job and you have built a following around it, then it's more than acceptable. However, many of us are associated with people, businesses, and organizations that expect us to safeguard their reputations through our social media usage. A good rule of thumb to use when checking if you should post something or not is asking yourself how well it will age. For example, in a year's time, will people still react positively to your post as they do now?

Chapter Takeaways

- Online privacy ensures that your identity and personal data is safe online. You can strengthen your online privacy by regularly checking and adjusting your privacy settings on apps and websites.
- Privacy is also crucial on social media, but even more important is protecting your mental health. Social media boundaries can help you set healthy social media limits so that you don't leave feeling drained or discouraged after spending time online.
- Social media boundaries can also protect you from being heavily influenced by unrealistic expectations or investing too much time in online relationships rather than maintaining real relationships.
- While it's good to express yourself on social media, be mindful of how your posts can be perceived by others. The type of content you post should be appropriate for each platform, and create a positive reflection of who you are.

10

Extra Exercises to Set Boundaries

"Hold yourself back, or heal yourself back together. You decide."

— BRITTANY BURGUNDER

This chapter talks about:

• Boundary building exercises to boost your confidence

Recognizing Boundary Violations

It's important to notice when a boundary has been crossed so you can communicate the violation clearly. Have a look at the tables below and make a note for each boundary violation you resonate with.

Communication Boundaries	
Violation	**Notes**
Texting, calling, or emailing excessively.	
Responding to you sarcastically.	
Yelling or raising their voice at you.	
Interrupting while you're speaking.	
Ignoring or minimizing your feelings.	
Others:	

Physical Boundaries	
Violation	**Notes**
Trying to isolate you from friends or family.	
Touching your body without consent.	
Going through your belongings without your permission.	
Denying your privacy.	
Standing or talking too closely.	
Others:	

Emotional Boundaries	
Violation	**Notes**
Constantly coming to you with bad news.	
Relying on you too much for emotional support.	
Failing to keep promises.	
Using humor in a demeaning way.	
Changing the topic or refusing to address your hurt feelings.	
Others:	

Control Your Urges

When a boundary has been violated, you might be triggered to act without thinking clearly about your decision. The following exercise will help you slow down your thinking and process your urges rather than acting upon them.

- **What do you have an urge to do?**

- **What boundary violation has triggered this urge?**

- **If you decide to give in to this urge, what will be the negative consequences?**

- **If you decide to control your urge, what will be the positive consequences?**

- **What coping strategies can you turn to as a distraction from the urge?**

- **Is there anyone you can speak to about your urge?**

Confronting Your Negative Beliefs

Your belief system reflects stories that you have told yourself about who you are and how safe it is to interact with the world and others. By recognizing thoughts that are harmful, you can pause and replace the thought with one that aligns with the kind of world you desire to live in. Below are examples of thoughts and the types of beliefs they reinforce. In the third column, write down a healthy replacement for the thought.

Thought	Belief	Replacement
Nobody understands me.	Overgeneralization	
My parents ruined my childhood.	Blaming	
I'm stupid and weak. That's why others take advantage of me.	Assumption	
If I get married, only then will people respect me.	Does not follow	
I feel betrayed. This friendship is over.	Emotional reasoning	
I don't need friends. I'm okay spending time by myself.	Relative deprivation	
If I raise an issue with my boss, they'll fire me.	Aggression as an argument	
They'll either respect me, or I'll cut them out.	Black and white thinking	
I'm judged because I'm different.	Mind reading	

Journaling About Your Feelings

Find a quiet room in the house or office where you can spend 20 minutes. Write about something that has been on your mind that you haven't spoken about. Don't worry about grammar, spelling, or punctuation—simply allow the pen to move on paper. Describe the emotional impact of this issue and the toll it has taken on your well-being. It's normal to get emotional during this exercise. Write as much as you feel comfortable sharing, then look over what you have written at a later time.

Responding to Threatening Communication

When you're communicating with an aggressive person, perhaps a family member or coworker, and they make threatening remarks that aren't true, it's important to stop them and challenge their opinions with your truth. Your truth is based on the positive perceptions you hold about yourself (i.e. your belief system and core values). When challenging threatening messages, focus on providing positive evidence from past experiences or what you know to be true about yourself.

Consider each threatening message written below and provide counterarguments that reflect your truth—the positive beliefs you hold about yourself. For example, if a friend said, "You wouldn't be able to do anything without me," you might respond, "The truth is I have a whole life outside of this friendship and my current goals are proof of that."

Threatening Message	Challenge
You will never amount to anything.	
You can't do anything right.	
That was such a stupid mistake.	
Do you listen with your ears?	
You need to fix the problem now, otherwise there will be consequences.	
Do you honestly think this is your best work?	
I think you're living in a fairytale. This is the real world.	
You need to try harder to impress me.	
I have never met someone so slow like you.	
Toughen up. Other people have it harder than you.	

Conclusion

Setting boundaries is one of those skills that's easy enough to explain, but difficult to put into practice. What makes boundaries tough to establish isn't necessarily that you don't know what you want, but instead that you're afraid of not getting what you need. You may be afraid of being turned down, ridiculed, or criticized for requesting others to respond to your needs.

It's possible that you didn't grow up in a household where there were any house rules, where adults behaved like adults, and where children were allowed to be children. As a result, you grew up without having a solid sense of self that could protect you from abusive or manipulative people you would meet as a young adult and well into your adult years.

The purpose of this book was to help you address that crippling fear and offer you the necessary tools to set healthy boundaries. However, even more than that, the strategies and exercises offered were designed to help you start believing more in yourself. The secret of communicating assertively, enforcing consequences, and knowing when to leave a relationship lies in having a high sense of self-worth. You need to believe without a doubt that you deserve feeling psychologically safe in relationships, voicing your opinions, and being shown the same respect you show others.

As you continue to practice setting boundaries, remind yourself that putting your needs first isn't selfish. It's an act of self-love. If you don't prioritize your needs, who will? Get comfortable with the process of setting standards with others and holding them accountable for their actions—yes, even those difficult family members or toxic coworkers. Setting boundaries will never stop being something that you do, because you're either meeting new people or discovering new needs from your relationships.

Therefore, make conversations about boundaries a common topic in your personal and professional relationships. Create an environment for open and honest communication about limits and expectations so that you leave very little room for misunderstandings. With time, you'll gain more confidence in standing up for yourself and teaching others how to relate to you.

Be patient with yourself; you'll start to notice your relationships becoming how you desire them to be. And if you're not able to rehabilitate a relationship, accept the situation and be willing to move on.

Thank You

I really appreciate you for purchasing my book!

You had the chance to pick a lot of other books, but you chose this one.

So, **thank you so much** for purchasing this book and reading it to the very last page! I hope that I was able to help you in your healing process, as my goal is to help as many people as possible!

Before you close the book, I want to ask for **a small favor**. Would you please consider *leaving an honest review* on Amazon about the book? **This would be really helpful for me**, as I'm an independent author and posting reviews is the best and easiest way to support me.

The feedback you provide will help me so I can continue selling, improving, and writing books. **It will mean the world to me to hear from you.**

Go to this book on Amazon and scroll down (https://mybook. to/set-boundaries), or scan the QR code to leave a review:

Amazon US —— Amazon UK —— Amazon CA —— Amazon AU

References

Amstel, B. (2019, June 9). *Individuation in therapy.* goodtherapy. https://www.goodtherapy.org/learn-about-therapy/issues/individuation

APA Dictionary of Psychology. (2022). Dictionary apa. https://dictionary.apa.org/dysfunctional-family

Eagle, J. (2011, December 1). *How to individuate.* Live Conscious. https://liveconscious.com/2011/12/how-to-individuate-step-one/#:~:text=If%20you%20want%20to%20learn

Eagle, J. (2011, December 2). *How to individuate. Learn the second step in this 3-step process.* Live Conscious. https://liveconscious.com/2011/12/how-to-individuate-step-two/

Hay, L. L. (2016). *Mirror work : 21 Days to heal your life.* Hay House, Inc.

Neff, K., & Dahm, K. (2015). *Self-Compassion: What it is, what it does, and how it relates to mindfulness.* In Springer. https://self-compassion.org/wp-content/uploads/publications/Mindfulness_and_SC_chapter_in_press.pdf

New International Version. (2011). Bible Gateway. https://ww

w.biblegateway.com/passage/?search=1%20Corinthians%201
3%3A4-7&version=NIV

Newsome, T. (2016, May 13). *Things more important than love in a relationship.* Bustle. https://www.bustle.com/articles/160
467-11-things-that-are-more-important-than-love-in-a-relat
ionship

Price, L. (2017, October 13). *9 Times stars shamelessly spilled other celebs' secrets.* People. https://people.com/celebrity/stars-
telling-other-stars-secrets/

Robinson, L., Segal, J., & Jaffe, J. (2021, February). *How attachment styles affect adult relationships.* HelpGuide. https://w
ww.helpguide.org/articles/relationships-communication/atta
chment-and-adult-relationships.htm

SCB. (2022). *Elon Musk's working style - Iron Man in the real world.* SCB. https://www.scb.co.th/en/personal-banking/stor
ies/success-story/elon-musk-working-style.html?hash_prima
ry=6772730A47BFEB83D5B792387B6168E4C32460AC#:~:t
ext=Works%20like%20a%20mad%20man

Solove, D. J. (2014, November 24). *Should celebrities have privacy? A response to Jennifer Lawrence.* TeachPrivacy. https://t
eachprivacy.com/celebrities-privacy-response-jennifer-lawre
nce/

Townsend, J. (2022, May 26). *How to determine the right conse-quences when setting boundaries.* Boundaries Books. https://ww
w.boundariesbooks.com/blogs/boundaries-blog/how-to-dete

rmine-the-right-consequences-when-setting-boundaries

Tygielski, S. (2017, February 9). *You stop attracting certain people when you heal the part of you that once needed them.* Shelly Tygielski. https://www.shellytygielski.com/you-stop-attracti ng-certain-people-when-you-heal-the-part-of-you-that-once -needed-them/

Also by Cher Hampton

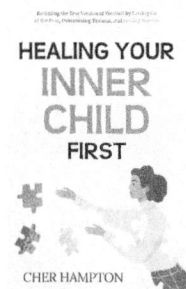

Healing Your Inner Child First

What to do with your past when it keeps on following you?

What comes to your mind when you hear the term "inner child?" Is it that you are carrying a child within (as in you are pregnant) or that it is a hypothetical version of yourself? This is just the tip of the iceberg you have touched, take a full dive in to get to know more about your inner child. **Yes! You have one too!** Everyone has an inner child.

No matter how old you are, everyone has a child within. You are your inner kid, but it is not the infantile mentality you have clung to all these years. It's your subconscious mind at work. It is *you* who possesses all your suppressed childhood memories and sentiments that return from time to time. **It's critical to your well-being and progress to heal your inner child FIRST.**

This book is an excellent resource for discovering your inner child. Not only that, but it also explains how to reclaim your inner child following any major or minor trauma, and how to do so in order to reach your full potential. **If you want to live a fulfilling life, you must not abandon this part of yourself.**

Printed in Great Britain
by Amazon

17229315R10108